LIFE AFTER CHRIST MAS

SELLING SUCKS. FIX IT!

Designed and Written by Dave Conrey
www.daveconrey.com

Edited by Michele Truty
www.micheletruty.com

Author Photography by Misha Hettie
www.mishahettie.com

ISBN 978-0-9904421-1-0

DEDICATED TO...

To you, the artists, designers, and makers who work tirelessly,
and sometimes thanklessly, to make cool things to share with the
world. Your value and self-worth is the *why* behind this book.

DON'T LIKE IT?
FIX IT!

This is the most unusual place for me to be putting content in the book, but I want to talk for a moment about the elephant in the room. You may or may not know this, but shortly after I published this book, I decided to change the design of the cover. The original design was adequate, got the message across, but it wasn't indicative of something I would typically design. To be clear, yes, I designed the original cover, and I was *satisfied* with the work, but it was made to be accessible for the masses. After listening to a few of my mentors talk on subjects of producing work that makes a difference, I went back to the design table to come up with a cover that better represented who I am as a creative.

I changed the cover because I should not compromise my work. My punk rock aesthetic comes from years creating flyers for friends; working with the limitation of proper design tools, and a high regard for the hardcore music I blasted while I worked. I cut my teeth on Art Chantry and David Carson (look 'em up), and gave conventional design the middle finger whenever possible... then life got in the way.

It's real easy to become complacent as a designer. We get used to churning out work that satisfies a client's needs, and we forget what it's like to make statement with our art. I spent ten years in magazine publishing where the work was more about production than creativity. This process burned a hole deep in my brain that creativity was not necessary. Expediency was far more appreciated than design prowess. So, when I went into designing this cover for who I thought might be my readers, I started with a concept that looked like what I thought people would read. This was a big mistake.

Of course you want to read this book for the content (which is quite kick-ass if I may say so myself), but you might also be reading the book because I wrote it. Perhaps you appreciate my outlook on business, and that's what makes you want to know my take on the subject. Or maybe you like this new cover design and can't help but want to know more about the dude behind it. Either way, my guess is that you are inspired by the attitude of this book, and not interested in books that cater to the masses.

I changed the cover because I could. I knew it wasn't working, so I fixed it. A good portion of this book talks about making adjustments to fix things that don't work, and to use your products and brand to speak to the world in the only way that you can. We are not put on this planet to be carbon copies of someone else, and we should never aim for the bloated middle ground. We have a voice and a style that only we can represent, and if we are not doing that 100% of the time, then we are not living to our full potential.

I changed the cover because I could, and because I want you to know you can do the same. Let's shake stuff up.

"Your playing small does not serve the world. There is nothing enlightened about shrinking so that other people won't feel insecure around you. We are all meant to shine as children do."

MARIANNE WILLIAMSON

TABLE OF CONTENTS

FOREWORD

When I was an emerging artist, success came hard and fast for me. Sales increased, my client list grew, and my potential opportunities were getting brighter every day. But for the first three to four years, it was an uphill battle. I would have a swell in business and get real comfortable spending extravagantly on expenses or new things, or take the family out more than a few times that week for dinner. I felt like it was Christmas day every day, with the sales coming in. Like I'd finally *arrived*.

Then Christmas actually happened. And soon after that? The surprise!

I was empty-handed, curled up in a corner crying myself to sleep. I couldn't figure out why everything changed so suddenly. Did I lose the interest of my collectors? Did the fans suddenly hate my latest offering? Was I doing something wrong in my marketing?

It wasn't long after that I understood the eternal roller coaster of being a retailer and artist. Learning how to work with the highs and lows would soon be comfortable, but budgeting where I could when sales were plentiful, so I could sit patiently and calmly during the dry seasons, was still quite tough. It was more than just budgeting, though. I had to change the entire way I dealt with my career, the way I ran business, and how I planned to reach my goals. It was all about the planning, the strategy, and the vision. You surely can't have strategy without vision, and with any business or career, it's vital to have goals and a strategy to get where you need or want to go. Even the top CEOs, wealthy tycoons, and sports stars have coaches and consultants. With a great support team, and the motivation of people like Dave, I was able to focus more clearly on my career and make things happen for myself, the way I wanted, with a consistent income to support my family.

This book is that perfect tool to help you, no matter what level of your career you find yourself, or what genre/craft of work you do. Back when I started, I wish I had the kind of advice and support that Dave shares with us in this book. If you want to learn how to create a consistent brand, build sustainable and evergreen income, sail the high tides of massive holiday sales seasons like Christmas, or even take advantage of the dry seasons, then this book is for you.

I've always been a fan of Dave Conrey's *Fresh Rag* blog and the podcast, as his teachings and one-on-one interviews are filled with powerful advice and personal experiences from creatives worldwide who have been there, just like you and me, huddling in the corner crying for mercy from the holiday slumps. This post holiday survival guide is truly an essential topic to get your hands on and get to know a little more. Take a hold of this oar that's being extended to you now, and dominate those tides!

- Natasha Wescoat, WescoatFineArt.com

INTRODUCTION

Here's how the scenario plays out for many creatives: You're running your business as you normally would on any summer day, but as you open the door to allow the warm breeze blow the curtains back, instead of a the familiar warmth of the past few months, you're hit with a brisk, cold shock instead.

Autumn snuck up on you, and as much as you might embrace the idea of the beautiful fall colors, you are stricken with anxiety. This cold snap means you have less than three months before the holidays and you haven't made enough product for the coming surge. You need to order supplies, get your workspace in order, put some calls into friends who may help you with the deluge, and then the overwhelm starts to hit. For a brief moment you think about all the money you'll make during the holidays, and it warms you up even though you will work your buns off during the entire season. But then you start thinking about the cliff your business drives off every winter, the depression you suffer because business slows to a crawl, and you've got more inventory than you know how to sell.

That inventory will sell throughout the coming year, but the clutter in your home only brings more anguish as you try to dance around the boxes and baskets of product, supplies, and shipping materials. That feeling gives you dread and you start to wonder if it's even worthwhile to make the effort. The holiday money is great, but the business of killing yourself for a few months in order to pursue what may feel like an expensive hobby starts to wear you down. Does it really have to be this way every single year? The short answer: No, it doesn't.

I've worked with dozens of makers, artists, designers, and other creative individuals on how to improve their position in the world, and what many of them regard as a necessary ebb and flow to the sales cycle of a handmade business, can be replaced with a consistent progression of sales.

All businesses suffer from some sort of slowdown after the holidays, but there are things you can do for you business to give it the strength to push through the post-holiday dropoff. It starts with a concentrated and consistent effort toward presenting your work and yourself to the community that would be your customers. Through a combination of branding, marketing, media interaction, customer service, and sales flow; you can build a business that is poised for growth from one month to the next.

In this book, we will tackle the details of branding, marketing, design, and sales, all within a schedule framework.

We'll Look at:
- Where to put your focus first
- How to prepare for the holiday surge, from Black Friday to December 24th
- How to ensure a refund-free New Year
- When the dust settles, how to maintain sales numbers through the coming months
- How to build a brand that people adore

One of the biggest changes will be in your mindset around branding, or as I like to refer to it, *everything you do with your business.* It really is that deep and important of a topic, and we'll discuss the subject at length. In fact, branding is the core element throughout these pages. You may think, *but I already have a logo,* and I will smile preciously at you for a moment before describing how branding is much more than a logo design and some pretty colors on your website. By the end of this book, you will have so many breakthrough moments about how to view your brand, aha may become your second-favorite word—the first favorite being *cha-ching.*

A large portion of the conversation will be around your approach to different media types, whether it's in print, featured on websites, or interacting on social media. I discuss how to establish a consistent message, including a unified visual identity, a storytelling mindset, and a specific vision of the ideal customer you want to serve.

Many creative sellers look at their business from a single-sale mindset, one customer at a time, hoping for a return visit with a coupon code. This strategy sometimes works, but you might be missing out on a chance to grow your business with simple efforts before, during, and after the transaction. What if you could create an opportunity where customers upgrade their purchase with premium options, or add multiple items to their cart? Sales can be fluid and natural, without being slimy. With the right sales approach, you create new chances for your customers to enjoy more of your work.

I also dig into how customer interactions can trigger a positive shopping environment, and what you can do to create a world that new customers are eager to be a part of. Here's a hint: It's more than just free shipping. In fact, it stems from a desire to give the customer a feeling of satisfaction, that even in the circumstance of a defective purchase, there can exist a rewarding experience. Sometimes that stems from top-notch customer service, and other times it comes from giving them all the answers they want before they ever need them.

In my book, *Selling Art Online*, I work to dispel the myth that there are only a handful of ways to make money as an artist. I'm proud of the book, and it continues to help new artists all the time, but because of the nature of the content, it has a shelf life. A majority of *Selling Art Online* talks about various places online where an artist can sell art, but the web being ever-evolving, that information changes constantly. Sites come and go with the tides, fall out of favor, or fail to stay relevant to their customer base. Even if a site is still prominent, their policies can change, creating a different scenario. Sometimes a site's business model changes, and it creates an entirely new dynamic, which may affect how your products get sold. When that happens, the information I've written about in the past may not be as relevant or valid. To keep it relevant, I must go back often to update it, or risk it being out of date.

When I started the concept of this book, I had the first one in the back of my mind. My goal here is to make this content as *evergreen* as possible; keeping the information relevant despite the changes in technology, business or public perception. I talk about all the big social media players like Facebook, Instagram, Twitter, and Pinterest, but the methods will transcend these platforms, and any platforms yet to come.

Life After Christmas is about creating sustainability, despite platform changes. This is not about the hot new sites or the best tactics of the year. Instead, it's about sticking to proven methods that work no matter what platform you are working on. Yes, there are unspoken rules to each, which should be heeded, but as long as you know those rules, you won't miss the capability to share and promote your work with style, grace, consistency, and sales success.

This book will give you the tools and knowledge that will sustain your business for years. I use the winter holidays as a framework because they are an ever-present thought in the minds of small business owners like you, but the methods in these pages are meant to be used to your advantage in any season. Follow the path and you will gain fans, add customers, and make money.

To make this work, you need to be clear about your purpose. It is possible for you to be successful working on projects that pay well but you're not passionate about. However, that is a hard hill to climb, and when you get to the top, there's always a another false horizon staring at you. When you pursue an easy buck over a strong purpose, the fulfillment of getting paid only lasts so long. Without proper motivation, you may grow to dislike the work, but you're stuck in it because it pays too good to quit.

I want you to make money! I want you to make lots and lots of money, because if you do, you'll tell everyone about the book that helped you get there. I also want you to be fulfilled and satisfied with the work you do. In fact, I want that more than anything. A big win for me would be you writing me an email in February telling me that you are kicking butt past the holidays, and you love every minute of your work.

That is my purpose for this book. Now, what's yours?

STOP!

If you're reading this book after the holiday season, you need to know a few things before you go further.

First, a lot of this guide is focused on the timing of things, especially in regards to the holidays. That said, this book is less about timing, and more about information you can apply to improve your daily work life. Even in the spaces where I talk about events that happen around the holidays, there is information that will be valuable to you after the new year.

Second, this is a combination of reference, business practices, and motivational guidance. I suggest you go through the book one time quickly, and then go back to hit specific sections that apply to you and your business at that moment. Absorb as much of the information as possible in the first round, and solidify the necessities by going over those details again.

Finally, there may be elements in this book that seem over your head, beyond your scope, or might not apply to your business at first glance. Please make an effort to read through them anyway because circumstances will arise where the information applies to something further along. If you hit a stumbling block, push through best as possible, because an answer may present itself.

Everything is figure-out-able, a Google search away, or just needs a little extra motivation to tackle. It's always easier to stop doing the hard work, and go about your business as usual, but as the idiom goes, "If you do what you've always done, then you get what you've always gotten." In other words, you will need to put forth the effort to make an impact, and it starts with a mindset of prosperity. You can do this, because others have done it before you, and at one time they were sitting right where you are now.

1

WHAT IS IT ABOUT THE HOLIDAYS?

There's something to be said about modern consumerism. We work all year just to spend our hard-earned cash on gifts for others in December. I'm not complaining, mind you, because I like presents just as much as the next guy who needs another fifty-inch television like a hole in the head, but it makes me wonder about our addiction to consumerism. What if we brought about an era where people buy things for others throughout the year, instead of bulking up between Thanksgiving and New Year's?

It's fun to celebrate with family and friends in grand fashion—go out with a big bang of escalating debt and fruit cake, but it's stressful to work most of your year at half-speed, and then push it to redline for three months. It's no wonder so many businesses crash into shut-down mode after the new year in anticipation of a long winter's nap.

Being a born and bred Californian, I have never had much need for seasons, and I admit my ignorance to the permanence of Ol' Man Winter breathing down your door for half the year. I can imagine it is easy to go into hibernation mode during those months, and come out around April or May to try and tackle spring, summer, and early autumn. I'm sure many reading this, possibly during a snowdrift, are over the never-ending winters we've had in the U.S. the past few years. It might be bad enough for them to kill a shiny-nosed reindeer for the chance at

Southern California sunshine and movie stars, but let me tell you something about the other side of that fence...

Californians don't know what hibernation means, and instead of spending holidays making popcorn garland and snow angels, we work on things. The sun is out, so why not do something productive? It's a great concept, really, and I enjoy the lifestyle, but for makers, it can be tough because sometimes there are no buyers for the products we make. We blew our marketing wad between October and December, using all of our energy to make the holiday season better than the last, which is never a guarantee.

We may have a load of cash in our pockets from holiday sales, but we might have taken a bit from the till to cover expenses, and now it's time to pay that back. If we're lucky, we have enough left over to help us get through the inevitable slow months. An who could forget April, when the tax man cometh for his pouch of shekels. Tapped out after that, what money is left for marketing at this point? Usually not much, thus we rely on our bootstrapping efforts and plenty of free social media.

I have a friend who sells greeting cards, and her mantra between October and February is, *Don't talk to me!* She does not want any interruptions during that time because she's busier than any human should be. She's lucky that Valentine's Day extends her holiday season a little longer than most sellers, but on February 15th, she collapses in a heap, with glass of ice in one hand and a bottle of Jim Beam in the other. Sometimes the glass isn't even necessary.

All of this got me thinking; what if we could build up the reputation of our business in a way that encourages customers to buy year round. What if our brand was so strong, people would clamor for it as much in March as they do in November? It's not such a foreign concept. If you look at corporate brands, those businesses work hard during the holidays too, but once the new year hits, they don't roll up into a ball and wait for the next selling season to come around. Instead, they go find the customers, and bring them back to the buying table.

Years ago, American Greetings and Hallmark knew the bulk of their business was between October and January. Instead of peeling back expenses in months when there was less business, they created business for themselves. Valentine's Day, Mother's Day, Father's Day, Grandparent's Day, Sweetest Day, Secretary's Day, and Boss's Day all came from the minds of the card companies. Do you think there's any coincidence that those all fall within the typically slow business months of the year?

Talk Like a Pirate Day started as a joke between friends, but now it's a phenomenon. Even if you don't know what day it is (September 19th), you know what it is. This unofficial holiday that started between two buddies is such a big deal, celebrities and big brands get involved. These two guys probably didn't think it would become a phenomenon when they started it, but you can sure bet they capitalized on the concept. They capitalized on a crazy idea, and now sell books and swag like crazy.

What special selling days do you have on your calendar? Black Friday, Small Business Saturday, and Handmade Monday? Indie makers put all their money on the table for a single weekend of selling, and hope the rest of the season follows suit. Any economist with half a mind would tell you that it's an insane approach to business, yet we do it every single year.

It takes a little more effort than inventing a few days during the year to get customers to buy in. You could tell buyers that April 10th is Crocheted Knickers day, and they may laugh at the concept, but will they buy? It takes more immersion than a Facebook post to get their attention, but with a concentrated effort toward brand building, interaction, storytelling, and well made products, you can build up enough support for your crazy ideas. Become a trusted source in the creative business space, and when you shout from the mountain top of your massive social media following that you declare June 19th as International Soap Maker's Day, people will pay attention.

The lesson here is not to speculate on the success of fictitious holidays, but rather, find ways to turn average days of the year into buying days for customers. Maybe you are using existing holidays to your advantage, or maybe every 1st of every month is the best day to buy because it's when you launch your one-of-a-kind items. The days don't matter as much as the depth of your message. The goal is to create year-round appeal with your work, and it starts with an effort to inform and engage our fans on a regular basis, or as I call it: Branding.

I believe everything we do that is witnessed by the public becomes a faction of our brand. I often refer to branding as the promise you make to people as they walk through your world. The future of your success begins and ends with that promise. Tell good stories, share nice photos, make high-quality products, and provide excellent service; those are the cornerstones. Make a compelling case of why people buy from you, and new customers will do so throughout the year.

Before we get deep into branding, it's important to establish what defines success for you. Moreover, what are the main characteristics of successful creative business owners, and how can we learn from them? Ninety-nine times out of one hundred, success stories are built upon a framework that anyone can follow. Once in a while, you get a fluke, an overnight success story, but the vast majority of successful individuals got there by repeating a series of proven techniques.

During the research phase of this book, I had the opportunity to talk to several creatives about the work they create. As I talked to these successful individuals, all at different stages in their career, I realized they all shared similar aspects of their work process, aspects that separate them from the people who struggle for success.

What I found with them is that success has nothing to do with what social media site you're on, which software you use, or what selling platform works best for your product or service. It's not about what famous people you align with, which conferences you attend, or the expensive training course you invest in. Instead, creative success comes from five key factors; every one of them within our reach, and it starts with identifying a need.

1. Find a Hole and Fill It

In my local community, whenever the city is doing roadwork that takes more than a day to complete, they put up signs that say OPEN TRENCH, which I find hilarious. If you think about it, *open trench* is a redundant statement, because of course, all trenches are open. Have you ever seen a *closed trench?* In truth though, there's something about the word open in that phrase that gives a sense of alertness to drivers. If the sign just said, trench, would we still be compelled to take caution? Would we be as keen to random holes in the road with reflective pylons and no sign?

I wonder if we are desensitized to our innate sense of caution because we rely on the powers that be to tell us when there is danger ahead. Perhaps because of that, we no longer can adequately spot potholes when they befall us. Perhaps the same goes for our business life. So many people go about their work following the paths of others instead of using their instincts to find the right way around a problem.

You may not look at your work and think that it's solving

a problem in the world, but it can solve a problem if you know where to look. Before you started on your journey, did you run across someone who was doing similar work, and you said to yourself, "I can do better than that." As a consumer, you felt there was a hole in the world for work similar to what you saw, except better. You identified a potential need in the market, and you took action on that idea.

If you've ever said to yourself, "I wish there was something that did this thing I need, but different," then you discovered a trench that needs filling. That's where real innovation happens. That's how smart phones and electric cars get made. It's how art goes from Van Gogh to Picasso, to Pollock, to Warhol, and so on. If we're not searching for those holes in the market, then we're missing an opportunity to shine.

Now, if you ever saw the work of someone else and said, "I could do that," and went out and made a carbon copy, then you didn't fill a need. Instead, you stacked your work on top of another person's trench. Sure, there might be space for two people to do what that person is doing, but are you differentiating yourself enough to stand out? If you can't answer that question with a resounding yes, then you didn't fill a hole.

In other words, don't be a closed trench. Go find an open trench to fill.

2. Believe in the Work

Successful creatives believe without a shadow of doubt that the work they do is the answer to someone's problem. They have a force within them that says, *This work matters, and I can't not do it.* A strong belief in the work you do is essential because it gives you drive, gives you purpose, and if you don't have the conviction to produce quality products or services, then you will never have the belief. Ironically, if you don't have the belief, you may never produce any work that matters. Without the belief, you will meander through life, searching for the the answers to your internal problem of putting pure, genuine, creative work out into the world, but never find the answers.

How do you expect anyone to clamor for your work if you can't show enough conviction to it yourself? You can't fake belief—it comes from within. If you've ever seen someone try to fake their way through a sales pitch, when you knew they didn't have the appropriate conviction, it shows. As they lose faith in their ability to sell the product, so goes your intention of buying, no matter how much you might want their product or service.

Play a game with me and finish this statement with complete honesty: "I believe my work is..." How you finish that sentence should give you an indication to your true belief. If it doesn't end with an amazing climax, then perhaps you need to question your motivation.

3. Believe in Yourself

We all have our moments of fear and self-doubt, and no one is free from the trappings of, *Am I good enough?* I saw an interview the other day with two prominent Internet entrepreneurs, and as they discussed their own stories, at one point they both acknowledged a fleeting case of impostor syndrome. Even as successful as they are in business, they still have moments when they feel like frauds, despite their heavy-hitter success.

Successful business owners know how to shake that feeling off, get back to work, and find the fire deep within that allows them to do the important work. To be a success, you must believe if yourself. You must believe in your capability, your talent, and most importantly, your message. At this moment, you should be asking yourself what you stand for, and how does your work support that belief?

The voice within you should scream, "I have no intention of stopping! I know I am good at this, and the world needs to see it." Without that fire, without that drive, the world will relegate you to the middle of the crowd, and you will never have an opportunity to step forward and shine. You must believe that if you do not succeed with your goal, the world will be less awesome, and therefore, you must succeed.

4. Desire to Learn and Grow

No one has all the answers. Even the most talented and famous people in the world have something to learn about doing good work. It's essential that you continue to learn and grow if you want to make a big impact in this life. Take more classes, read more books, find mentors to follow, and become a student of the game.

Back in my early twenties, I meandered through life, not sure where I was headed. I dropped out of college because I wasn't inspired by what I was studying, I took a job as a bartender, and my world revolved around making tips. Those tips would get spent back at another bar, like some strange, destructive circle of life. I remember one day picking up a copy of *Entrepreneur* magazine, back when it was filled with all kinds of crazy money-making schemes, making my head spin with curious interest and dreams of riches. Even back then, I was craving an entrepreneurial lifestyle, and I dove into that magazine, looking for the one thing that would make me rich.

I bought into a windshield repair program, not because I was passionate about the subject, but because it was a small investment, and there was a promise of making tons of money on this new technology. I was eager to get started, so I charged headfirst into it. I knew I needed to operate professionally, which meant I needed a logo and some business cards. I didn't know how to go about buying a logo from a designer. I didn't even know what graphic design was back then, but I had a computer at home and figured I could buy software and figure it out.

I got my hands on a copy of CorelDraw, the program of choice for amateur and professional illustrators alike before Adobe took over the top spot. I fumbled my way through the program until I was happy with a logo that represented my work. I don't have that logo anymore, and I'm sure it is atrocious, but after that effort, I was hooked. I still didn't know what graphic design was, but I was designing things for people just because I could. I bought magazines on the subject, read books, learned things online, and before I knew it, I had started a fledgling design career. That was nearly twenty years ago, and ever since then, I have had a voracious appetite for consuming information to help me improve my life, improve my career, and do what I can to make an impact on this world.

If we do not support ourselves with continuing education, we are saying that it's OK to go through life relying only on our current knowledge base, which is pretty dumb. The world is always changing, and if you do not change with it, you will get left behind. Your next level of success comes from a desire to learn more. Take a class, join a mastermind group, or just go hang out with people smarter than you. Make it a preoccupation to find ways to absorb new information, but new information is only as good as its execution, which leads me to the last point.

5. Take Action

You may have the best intentions in the world, but without the desire to put those intentions into action, your dream will remain a dream. You must take action on your plans. Maybe you don't have an organized plan yet, and maybe you're not sure which direction to take toward your goal, but none of that matters as much as taking a single step in any direction.

Have you seen those shoes the kids wear that light up when they walk or run? The harder they run, the more the lights blink, creating a visual spectacle as they tear across the playground. I once saw a young girl donning a pair, cautiously following her mother through a department store. Her shoes hardly lit up as she finessed her way across the ground where she stepped. It wasn't until she rounded the corner, when the toy section came into view, that she jumped up to let her mom know she wanted to go look at the toys. The lights on her shoes blinked away as she jumped, and when her mom sent her off into toy nirvana, her feet glowed like tracers shooting across the wide open lane of the department store floor.

For you, the bright light in your work will not shine unless you jump up and race toward your goal. Until you take action, all your positive thoughts and beliefs will remain empty. Find a point of entry, take a step, and make progress toward something, anything. Even if you do head in the wrong direction for a while, some forward momentum is better than none.

I recall a statement by a woman whose name escapes me, but the quote went something like, "As you stand on the edge of the abyss, wondering how you will cross the chasm into greatness, there are only two scenarios we must consider. When you step forward, you either have faith there will be something to stand on, or when you step into the emptiness, you will learn to to fly."

Find a place to plant your flag, believe, learn, grow, and take action. Do those things and you will become better at what you do.

MAYBE CHRISTMAS ISN'T YOUR THING

Not everyone's business clock works on the winter holiday schedule. If you're a fashion designer, your schedule started long before Christmas. If you sell plants and seeds, then you're waiting for the snow to thaw before you ramp up to full speed.

Although I use the winter holidays as a guideline for the lessons in the book, what you learn in these pages relies less on the actual calendar than on the method of creating a strong year-round push of your work. Christmas and Chanukah are the big ones, for sure, and Black Friday is as ubiquitous to shopping as tryptophan, football, and fights between inebriated family members. We cannot ignore the significance of the winter holidays, thus the title of the book, but for every reference I make to Christmas and New Year's, keep in mind your timeline and how to apply the lessons.

Ideally, you walk away from this book with renewed spirit and energy that keeps you pumped and moving regardless if it's November or June. As mentioned earlier, no matter when you pick up this book, and how that relates to your schedule, you can apply these lessons today to get you started in the direction of your big, fat, hairy dream.

You will always have your seasons, but you do not run a seasonal business. Together, we are challenging the status quo on what makes a great brand. In that, you get a new perspective on how to build and grow. It will be a lot of work, and it may require you to shift your mindset, but if you use the methods in this book, you will see consistent growth. Do the work, and I guarantee this will be one of the most memorable journeys of your entire business life.

MORE THAN JUST A LOGO

Let's be a little scandalous for a moment and talk about someone you know. Actually, it's someone we all know. You know when you go to a party or gathering and that one person shows up who just lights up the room? They walk in, and everyone is excited to see and talk to them. They dress great, have great hair, charisma for days, and people want to hang out with them. This person exudes confidence, is friendly with everyone, and is conversational with anyone in the room. They are an anomaly, rare as a red diamond and just as brilliant.

When that person came into the room, what you witnessed was branding at its purest, most effortless level. That level of branding is the holy grail of marketing, but how can less impressive humans like ourselves achieve that level when it's not ingrained in our DNA? Simple—study the formula.

Most might not put branding as the top reason for their sales success, but this is where I believe a lot of companies go wrong. If sales is the engine that keeps the business vehicle in motion, branding is the weld that holds the machine together. Branding is also the fuel, engineering, navigation, radio, and sparkly paint. In other words, branding is everything you do in your business that surrounds your sales.

One of my clients asked me which aspects of branding they should spend the most energy on for their business. My universal answer to this question is all of them. It takes work to get your branding in motion, but once you do, and you're diligent, branding operates like a well-tuned machine. Ignore any portion, and you may still get yourself down the road, just not at the same pace as the sports car in the lane next to you.

It's important to note that there are many interpretations to branding, and I express my personal views based on my research and experience. Others will differ, and maybe disagree, but after talking with numerous creative professionals, the ones who make the biggest impact have the the the most cohesive branding strategy, and it includes everything from their words and online presence, to their color choices and imagery.

While we're on the subject of imagery, many people assume when I say branding that I am talking about logos, business cards, and website headers. These items are all part of your brand, no doubt, and a strong logo is important to a strong brand, but aesthetics are only a tiny portion of your entire brand. In fact, your logo and color choices have less to do with the overall appeal of your brand than the way you serve and share. Provide tremendous value and your logo will enhance the brand. If you're not nice, or have poor service levels, there is nothing a beautiful logo can do for you.

A person who comes in contact with your brand for the first time will make a determination about you from that first interaction. If your logo sucks, that may hurt a little. However, if they found you because of an interesting photo you shared, or a useful article you wrote, and then saw your logo, they will be more inclined to stick around. Should you have a great logo and cohesive color palette across your marketing collateral? For certain, but the real task you have in front of you is stitching those threads into the tapestry of your brand. Every single thing you've said or done with your company made some impact on someone about who and what you are about. If your customer retention rate is low, then there's a branding problem. If you have repeat customers, but they never buy your higher-end products, then you have a branding problem. The goal is to identify those holes in the tapestry and fix them.

As we dig deeper into this subject, you will become acutely aware to all the opportunities you might have missed. From this moment forward, you will sweat the small stuff more. There's a lot of small stuff to tackle, and that's ok, because sometimes good business is made in the small stuff. That said, don't let that small stuff keep you from making projects happen. As you make tweaks to your branding. The public opinion of your brand will grow stronger, and you will find the customer retention you desire. The small stuff can be tedious, but reap big rewards if you stick to them.

A BRAND DEFINED

In the past two decades of working as a marketing and design professional, I have heard many interpretations of the term *branding,* but most do not resonate with me. For instance, the American Marketing Association defines branding as, "a name, term, design, symbol, or any other feature that identifies one seller's good or service as distinct from those of other sellers. The legal term for brand is trademark. A brand may identify one item, a family of items, or all items of that seller. If used for the firm as a whole, the preferred term is trade name."

Not only is that boring, it misses the mark in my opinion. In their definition, they reduce branding down to a small aspect of a company's visual statement. This is exactly why some people believe a logo, a font combination, and a color palette make up a brand, but that's wrong.

Jeff Bezos of Amazon is famed for stating, *Your brand is what they say about you when you're not in the room,* and I agree with this to a point, but it puts a very ominous label on the term, and also asserts that you have little control over how your brand is perceived. I believe we have a greater control over our brand perception now more than ever, and we can craft that effort with precision. It's when we don't pay attention to how the brand is managed that the ship goes adrift.

I believe branding is the promise you make to people as they walk in your world. Whether they have only seen a glimpse of you on Twitter, or they have gone through your entire sales process, the emotional attachment they make to your brand is based on every single touch you make. A tweet can define your brand as much as a package in the mail. Each small effort made, from steps one to one hundred and beyond, creates an impression upon your fans and customers.

In Christmas of 2013, my wife bought me an Kindle e-book reader. Being a sausage-fingered ruffian who likes to fumble delicate, electronic devices, my first instinct was to find a case for the new machine for fear of dropping it repeatedly on the hardwood floor. The irony of this is that since I bought a case, I have not dropped it once, but I digress.

My first search was on Amazon, naturally, but nothing there had the aesthetic I wanted. I turned to Etsy and found plenty of handmade device covers, but like many *crafty* items, most were not meant for manly men such as myself. Sailboats, butterflies, and happy faces are not really the image I want to portray when I show off my Kindle to the world. Of course I'm secure in my masculinity, why do you ask?

To be honest, I didn't need something overly masculine, but quality design was a priority. I came across a nice felt and leather piece by Byrd and Belle, a case design company run by independent designer Angie Davis. The display image of the felt case atop a wooden background appealed to my manly nature, but something about the composition of the image got my attention to dig deeper.

Inside Davis' shop, I found an array of similar well-composed images featuring various bags and cases. Her Etsy shop is one of the most attractive shops I have ever seen, and I was impressed with her visual execution from one listing to the next. Digging deeper, her secondary images completed the story, and although I needed to read the details, I knew I had found the case I was looking for. It was pricier than some others on Etsy, but I knew without a doubt, because of Davis' attention to the design and imagery, that her product would be high-quality. I plunked down my credit card, made my purchase, and high-tailed it out of there quick before I spent money I didn't had on more of her products.

Since the item was made on demand, it took several days to receive, which I knew going in because Davis made that clear in the listing. Instead of the instant gratification of buying something mass-produced on Amazon, I felt proud that I was buying something of quality, made to order, and it would be in my hands as soon as she finished the last stitch. When the delivery driver dropped the box on the porch and pressed the doorbell, I jumped up to see my purchase. I was not disappointed.

The box alone looked special, and as I cracked open the package, I was greeted with one small treat after another. The whole presentation of the packaging and the delicate placement of collateral on top of the case made my design sensibilities tingle. This indulgence of beautiful presentation was design porn if I ever saw it. From the care taken with the packaging, to the finely crafted receipt, and the collateral that matched the brand, this was the most bacchanalian of design orgies. Of course the product itself was as high-quality, as expected, but before I even had a chance to look at the case closely, I dropped it on the table and ran over to my computer to send Davis an email. I wanted her on my podcast right away. You can check that one out at www. freshrag.com/ftv3, if you're interested.

That's how powerful branding can be. I went from a customer to an evangelist in the time it took me to open a box. Davis knows by now that I would jump at the chance to share Byrd and Belle's goods. She treats her cases as if she was the only person on earth making them. Hundreds of cases a month get made in her shop, and it's not because she has a popular blog, or a huge social media fan base. It's because Byrd and Belle make quality products and showcase them in a way that's unmatched. Now there are people who are trying to bite her style, but it's too late. She's made the list of some of the best tastemakers, who are driving traffic to her shop by the thousands. As long as Davis continues to put together the best quality work, and showcase her product in the way she does best, there will be no end to her success. Byrd and Belle is brand mastery in its highest form, and it's something you can emulate if you put the time and energy into creating a system that works for your products or services.

Not everyone can use the Byrd and Belle method to their advantage, but it's a good start. The important factor to note is how you can take the simple and small aspects of your business process and change them up to create a long-lasting impression with your fans and customers. Where packaging and presentation are Davis' strengths, yours might be in how you tell the story of yourself and your products. Or maybe you create a system of top-notch customer service and satisfaction that people begin shopping with you strictly because they know they are going to get that level of commitment. It can be difficult as a small business owner to manage every aspect of your business with this type of precision, poise, and elegance, but pick an area of expertise, build upon that theme, and you can create that lasting impression one customer at a time.

THE NFL'S BRANDING PROBLEM

Ever since my wife and I decided to kill our standard cable in lieu of video streaming services, I don't watch sports that often, especially football. It's not a priority for me, and the longer I go without watching any, the less I care. Considering recent events about the NFL's scandals (which could be just about anytime in recent history), I'm not inclined to watch.

The way the NFL is dealing with their player problems is putting a large, ugly stamp on the organization that no amount of slick marketing or advertising will cure. No fancy font and color palette combination will supersede the story that they are telling the world with their actions, or inaction, as the case may be.

In 2014, the league tried to sweep the Ray Rice domestic abuse incident under the carpet, hoping it would go away, but a leaked video to TMZ.com changed all of that. Under fire for not taking action when they should have, the NFL laid down severe punishment with a massive stroke in order to save face and assume some sort of culpability for Rice's actions. In that same week, Adrian Peterson of the Minnesota Vikings was called out for disciplining his children with abusive techniques. At first got a slap on the wrist, but after pressure from the fans and media, the NFL laid down an indefinite suspension.

Back at the turn of the twenty-first century, Ray Lewis, retired veteran of the Baltimore Ravens, was a two-count murder suspect, but there wasn't enough evidence to convict. At the start of the 2014 season, the Ravens honored Ray Lewis with a statue outside the stadium for his contributions on the field. Sure, the fans loved it, but the rest of the world gasped in a collective, WTF? Pete Rose, one of the greatest ball players in history, is banned from baseball indefinitely because of gambling, but Ray Lewis gets a statue?

No matter where your opinion falls on these situations, the story the NFL is telling the world is they are soft on the actions of their players right up until the point of heavy public scrutiny. Only then will they take action. Past indiscretions are brushed away, and those players who have beaten, raped, or even killed others can still be treated like heroes. This scenario seems to play out year after year, and as more disenfranchised fans move away from standard cable, the league will continue to suffer.

How you manage the ugly parts of your business is just as important as how you manage the pretty things. Go ahead and sweep the ugly under the carpet, but if anyone finds out about it, you're in for a wild ride of public disdain. If instead you have a plan in place to manage the ugly situations in a way that is commiserate with the vision of your brand, should a situation arise, you'll have set actions you can perform to manage it.

You probably don't have rogue employees laying down physical harm on others like the NFL, but maybe you have a packaging and shipping snafu that needs fixing. Perhaps you have a disgruntled customer who is shouting their displeasure all over social media. What is your contingency for that scenario? Many large corporations now have staff dedicated to tracking down just such scenarios, equipped with plans and actions for those situations.

Your brand is the sum of the good stuff and the bad stuff, and if you don't have a plan in place for when surprises come up, your customers will ultimately manage your brand for you. Screw up someone's order and take a passive or distant approach to handling it; they will tell the world that you are passive and distant. If instead you manage the situation with poise and elegance, they may tell the world about your regal posture. Good news often goes unspoken, but bad news always gets shouted from the rooftop.

So, what does the NFL do from here? I'm sure the tonnage of intraleague bureaucracy they need to manage is staggering, but if I were commissioner, the first thing I would do is denounce all unsavory behavior. Domestic abuse, drug usage and criminal behavior gets a zero-tolerance policy. I'd create a fierce code of conduct for players and staff that becomes a public record. I'd also create a fan bill of rights that creates a level of expectation every team, and every player must sign.

The short story is that the NFL cannot control what players do in their free time, but until they better manage how to deal with problems that arise, NFL players will continue to rank right up there in public opinion with politicians and Catholic priests.

FUNDAMENTALS OF A UNIQUE EXPERIENCE

When it comes to branding, it's good to understand the framework of what makes a solid brand. This is up to interpretation depending on who you hear it from, but since you're here, listening to me, we'll go with my method for now. I break this method down into four categories: storytelling, public relations, customer experience, and aesthetics. As I deconstruct each one of these areas, keep in mind the nuances between them. Nothing here is mutually exclusive unto itself, and it takes a cohesive effort of all these elements to create an elegant, professional, and trustworthy brand.

On the flip side, nobody should be expected to tackle all of this at once and make it work. The rare marketing genius might be able to pull it off. My suggestion is to note the sections where you shine the most and see if you can improve upon them. Once you feel good about those areas, start integrating more bits into your repertoire as you grow.

Even the largest and most robust companies around have a difficult time handling every aspect of branding with precision, and they have several staff members, if not whole divisions, working on it. Don't be too hard on yourself if you can't juggle it all. Work your strengths, add in new items as needed, and do the best you can to stick to your plan. Maintain it to the best of your ability, and your customers will love you for your truth and effort.

THE PERFECT CUSTOMER

Sometime in the past few years, the chosen terminology for a perfect customer went from a *demographic,* to a *target market,* and is now often referred to as an *ideal customer avatar* (ICA). When I first heard the new term, it sounded a little *woo-woo* to me, but the deeper I got into it, the more I realized it is an essential phrase for any business owner, especially one who makes their living through creativity.

The difference between a demographic and an ICA is depth. Demographics deal with generalities like age, sex, location (instant mental time warp back to AOL circa 1999), but they don't get much deeper than that. Demographics relate to groups of people, and the methodology deals in broad spectrum. That can be acceptable to a point, but in a day and age where everyone is becoming more intimate with each other via social media, broad spectrum isn't going to cut it when it comes to making a connection with people.

An ideal customer avatar is more than general reference to a group of individuals. The point of an ICA is to tap into an individual, as literal to that term as you can muster within your own creativity. The exercise allows you the chance to take your imagination and get intimate with this individual who buys everything you sell, and tells all their friends in the process. Getting this straight in your head at the beginning will make the rest of the marketing you do go a lot smoother because you have a mental picture of that person who buys your products or services.

PROCESSING IMAGINARY DATA

The first step in figuring out your ICA starts with the target market you have now. If you don't have a clear idea of that target, take the most common denominators of the customers you've had interaction with, and use those as a starting point. You'll want to note the commonalities in demographics, age, sex, location, family dynamic, work status, industry, etc. Add to that the philosophical, psychological, and religious beliefs, along with the hobbies and interests of those customers, and you're off to a good start with establishing your ICA, but you still have work to do.

Taking those elements into consideration, start molding them into a human form. Try to understand their behaviors, buying habits, what motivates them to pick one item over another.

Imagine sitting across a table from them and asked them all the questions you ever wanted to ask about their reasons for buying. You have the opportunity to create this person from the ground up. They should be rational and real, but you can also create their story yourself. The method for getting the information together is far less important than the end result. You're establishing a reason to turn your marketing efforts toward this individual. Make it worth your while to paint the most elaborate picture possible to get the story you need.

There is one caveat here, and it's a difficult one to get past, because what I'm about to tell you will go against your natural instinct. Do NOT make this person out to be you. At some level, part of you will be in there, because you are using your own frame of reference to manifest this individual. When you got into your business, it was because you saw a gap in the market that you thought you could fill, and if you see that gap, others should too, and want to buy from you. At least that's the typical rationale, and it's why most people who go through this exercise end up with an ICA that is similar to themselves. Don't do that! Find your way toward someone more developed, and original, one that has traces of you (because you buy things too), but doesn't end up as your döppleganger.

Before you launch yourself into a marketing frenzy focused at this person, you need to ask this last question. Think about this individual and ask yourself, is this the customer you want, or is this the one you already have? You are using your personal frame of reference too much. If this ICA you created is not the person you want, then how do you get them there? If the gap is in their budget for discretionary spending, what kind of financial situation do they need be in to get to that desired income? If it's a philosophical standpoint, what needs to change to get them on board with your point of view? Redevelop this person to fit the type of customer you need them to be.

If you don't get this nailed down, you will spend all your energy pitching your work to the wrong person. You will have a mindset about the person you think is buying your work, and not about the person who should buy it. You will talk to them as the person they are, not the person they should be, and you will get exactly the customer you created. Find the holy grail of customers, and develop your ICA around that ideal. That is where the money exists.

STORYTELLING

In the past, what I would call storytelling is now what I refer to as branding. Storytelling is the basis for establishing your personality and point of view on the world. It's through that storytelling that you will find commiseration and kinship with people who believe what you believe. When you find people who believe what you believe, they will likely buy things that you sell because it also represents what they appreciate.

When I say storytelling, I don't mean that you have to put together words and phrases in prose-like fashion in order to craft a tale that intrigues and entertains. To some degree you do, but nobody is asking you to be the next Stephen King, J.K. Rowling, or James Patterson. The act of putting a little bit of your personality into each blog post, Twitter update, Instagram photo, or Etsy product description is enough to give the fans a better idea of the human on the other side of the words they are reading.

The point is to be as consistent as possible, while remaining true to your nature. Perhaps writing a blog post is against your nature, and the thought of sharing your life in that arena scares you to death. Storytelling does not have to be a blog, a podcast, or video. Storytelling can be done in photos, graphics, quotes, or the content you share of others. The links you share on Twitter, photos you reblog on Tumblr, or images you pin on Pinterest can say as much about you as the work you do. It's a little different when you're not expressing your own words and work, but there's a personality in everything you put out there. The more you do it, the better your chance of reaching your core customer.

When it comes to storytelling, the message counts far more than the medium. For me, writing and podcasting are my strengths, so I share my work those ways most often. I do dabble in photos, graphic quotes, occasionally videos, but I am most comfortable using spoken and written words. Choose what fits you best, and do not be swayed by what others are doing. Just because your competition does well in video, does not mean you must do the same. Below are a few of the options to consider.

Blogging

Many people will tell you that you absolutely need a blog no matter what, and in the past, I might have agreed, but I know plenty of people who are successful now without operating a blog. Could they get more reach with a blog? Sure, but it's not an imperative. There's also nothing that says you can't use your blog to only showcase photos of your work, perhaps accompanied with a few descriptive words about the piece. Your blog does not have to be filled with diatribes of text in order to resonate with people. If you're a writer, great, but that is not a requirement

Another thing to consider about having a blog is that if you are writing quality content that people link to and share, that will help you rank higher in the search engines. Search engine optimization is an uphill batter, but links can help you get more reach.

Guest Posting and Interviews

Occasionally you will come across someone who runs a website and wants to share you or your work on their site, whether that's a guest-posting opportunity, a curation of your work, or an interview. These are great opportunities for growth, but you need to be mindful about venturing into this space. Guest posting in someone else's space is not something to take lightly. You want to write your absolute best work here, keeping with the tone of their site while mixing in your personality. It can be a tricky balance, but if you're aware, you can pull it off with precision. The last thing you want is to portray yourself a certain way to their readers, but when they click through to your site, they find a different person. As long as you can maintain your style and voice, there won't be a disconnect with the fans.

Interviews are easier, depending on the type and style of the interview, but be mindful to stay informative and entertaining without being self-congratulatory. With guest interviews, you're at the whim of the publisher, and you never know how the end result with play out until it's posted. The same goes for curated posts of your work. The possibility for a wider reach can happen big with certain sites, but don't chase the numbers just for the sake of getting more clicks. You need to make sure the sites you approach, or approach you, are aligned with your own story.

Photo-telling

Telling stories through photos is becoming more popular amongst the creative set. Using Instagram, Pinterest, Tumblr, and Flickr can grow your fan base, but you need to consider your point of view closely. First, you need to have top-notch photos. You don't need to be a pro, but if you post up crappy, generic photos of overused themes, nobody is going to pay attention. If you only share your work, and nothing about your interests and personality, no one will care. The most popular people on Instagram are those who follow a simple process of producing quality work, letting that work tell a story, and are true to themselves as a creative source.

If your family is a large part of who you are, and you don't mind sharing photos of your kids, then show all those embarrassing photos they will likely hate you for in the future. Whether you like wilderness, street art, gardens, high-quality food, airplanes, or whatever your passion, put that passion out into the world. The more you can tie the passion into your work, the better. As long as you strive for beautiful images your fans can relate to, there are no rules. Snap away and let the world know what you like most in photographic form.

Email Newsletter

This is another subject we will go into great detail later, but for now, know that you very much should have an email list. Perhaps you don't know what to talk about in your email list, and that may keep you from starting one, but believe me when I say that there is no more engaged group of individuals than your email list. They have openly invited you into their inboxes, and that's as close to a personal connection you can get with a stranger who exists only online.

Also, in the battle for space and attention, when you have a list that is yours and yours alone, that means you will never be left in the cold. Your website could implode, your shop could be shut down, or you could get banned from Facebook for posting too many elbow pictures that look like boobs (true story), but that email list will always be there. Your Etsy shop could shut down tomorrow—without a list, how would you tell your fans you were ramping up a new shop? If you had a list, you could send out an email that day telling people that you have a new shop and that they should find you there. Instead of a halt to progress, you would notice hardly a blip on the radar of sales interruption. So, go start a list right now. There's a resource list in the back of this book with links to various email autoresponder companies you can use.

About Page

Although seemingly frivolous and indulgent, the About page of any site is typically the second most visited page, after the home page. People get the initial gist of what you're about, and then move right over to the About page to find out what's really going on. Now you have a chance to woo them, but this is no time for indulgences. This is where you set the tone of all that you do with your work.

When thinking of what to write for your About page, remember that it's not about you, but rather, what you can do for the reader. When they visit your About page, they want to know why they should even be there, and it has nothing to do with your bio. They want to know what they will learn, what the will get, or what they can buy from you. When you write your first words for your about page, they should be in a style that matches your own, while explaining that the site is all for them.

Once you have accomplished that portion, then you can write your bio, because some people may care where you came from and what you're about, but this is less important that letting them know why they should stick around.

PUBLIC RELATIONS

The way we manage our presence online in various media outlets can sway public opinion greatly from one direction to the next. Whether it's social media, press interviews, or direct customer interaction, the way in which we speak can help or hurt our branding efforts, and depending on the sentiment, the opinion can flip on you in an instant.

I refer to this group of branding elements as public relations because this is where the public will find you most often, and determine your value in a short, initial impression. Does that mean be tight-lipped and calculating with your words? No, not any more than you would be completely candid and forthright with your feelings and opinions publicly, but it does mean that you should consider your words carefully. Staying on message is important, as well is knowing when to come off message in a way that still tells your story.

Social Media

There are some out there that use social media as their outlet for all the crazy stuff that goes on in their heads. There are also some who have a hard time sharing anything remotely personal for fear of privacy concerns. There is no one single right way to use social media for your business, and only you can determine your comfort level. That said, there is a strong chance that a conservative comfort level in social media may be keeping you from reaching a wider and deeper audience.

Your job on Twitter, Facebook, and other sites is to make sure what gets said is inline with your point of view in life and business. The way you express yourself in these mediums should reflect how you would be if you were sharing them live, in person. There are tactics and techniques (tacniques?) that you can use to your advantage, like post frequency, link placement, and hashtags, but really, the story is the important element. You can find success with an aggressive social media campaign, but is that genuine to your nature, or just a tactic?

You know those times when a celebrity gaffs on Twitter and the world erupts? Britney Spears gets an embarrassing photo snapped, and for the rest of her life, people will remember her shaved head swinging an umbrella at a paparazzi. You and I may not have the public scrutiny of Britney Spears, but within our own circles, we can still have an impact. Do you want that impact to be a false representation of who you are, or a reflection of your natural identity?

Also, remember to use each social media platform individually. The way you talk to people on Twitter is not how you talk to them on Facebook, and not how you talk to them on Google+. You can share the same message across all channels, but go in speaking the language, or risk a disconnection with your people.

The social media world you dabble in is not the real world, which means you do not have be the real you. Your messages should be real and authentic, but they can be selective too. Someone once shared with me the acronym D.T.S.S. which expands to Don't Tweet Stupid Stuff. That's pretty much the overarching point of view for this next section.

Groups and Forums

Although groups and forums are a faction of social media, I put them in a different category because of the deeper impact they can have on your brand's appeal. These pages can be used in a variety of ways, but what I have found to be the most effective approach is to be a resource for others. Become a shining light in the lives of others, and the reverie will follow you back to your shop.

I do not hang out in groups and forums too much, though. Very often, they can spur a hive mentality around subjects, often negative, and I don't have time in my life to waste reading the disdain of others. Forums and groups can be valuable silos of informations, so when I do visit, I go into a group to either pose a question, or share a positive story that I believe will uplift others. If I have a question, I use the search function to see if the information has been shared before, get the info, and then thank the original poster for sharing. If the question has not been answered, I make my statement quick and get out of there, allowing time for people to answer. Forums have this magical ability to tractor-beam you in and keep you in its grasp by reading one engaging post after another, so beware. It's easy to get caught up in busy procrastination. There's not enough time in the day to waste it in these places.

If I am in a sharing mood, I will go in to a group or forum and look for questions posed that I may be able to answer. If I find a few to hit up, I'll spend a few moments interacting, but I steer clear of drama, and I get out quick. I want to be a resource for people, but I still have work to do, and it's not happening in these groups. Get in, get help, be helpful, and then get back to work.

Media Attention

At some point, if you're doing good work, someone is going to want to share your story with others. In the beginning, any press is good press, and it's important to get your message out there, but I believe a measured approach is the best approach. Spreading your press love around over time will help keep your name in circulation. Getting featured on the occasional blog, or doing an interview throughout the year will bring a consistent traffic source to your business.

Sometimes you may have a flash of interest, perhaps because you were found by a popular media outlet, and the rest of the world took notice. You may get swarmed with requests of your time, and it will feel awesome to have so many sources banging down your door for attention, but a consistent, season-beater business happens because you are working, not chatting about the work. The work may include an interview, but if you're spending all your time giving your story to another outlet, then the real work isn't happening, and that could affect the downline, which could backfire on you because customers aren't being handled.

Having too many people chase you down for your attention can be a good problem to have, but using the press to your advantage is the key. Pick and choose your media outlets wisely, and if you can put off some for another week or month, then do that. Spread the love around throughout the year as much as possible and it will bring long-lasting results.

If you're not getting that many knocks on your door, then by all means, indulge the ones you get. Remember that they want to see you in your brightest light, but you gotta be you. Just as in any other space, the world you will be exposed to through a story or interview should share the most true and authentic version of you. When people read the interview, they should feel like they met the person face to face... in case they ever do meet you face to face. It's easier to perpetuate the story that way.

CUSTOMER EXPERIENCE

For years, I have contended that the best marketing effort you can make is stellar customer service. It's more than just how you deal with the questions and concerns, but rather, the entire experience a customer has with your business, even if you are not directly involved. Right at this moment, there could be someone looking at your site and making a determination about you based on what they are seeing. There's nothing you can do about turning that anonymous person into a buyer, or is there?

If branding is the promise you make to people as they walk through your world, then their experience as a customer is essential. How you trigger the senses is crucial, and it starts from the moment they click your link. Aside from the obvious visual elements, how are people welcomed into you world?

The Buying Process

The way someone travels, from the moment they step into your site, to the moment they click the Buy Now button, they are making a determination about you. Again, consistent message is key, and personality goes a long way toward encouraging trust in potential customers. The words you use in your copy, the policies you keep, and the ease of getting from one step to the next all play a part. Even the receipt you send provides an opportunity for making a life-long customer. They may have bought from you, but did you leave them empty at the closing? Sure, they will enjoy the thing they bought from you, but were you so memorable they are compelled to share you with everyone?

Technology can play a big part in this, and sometimes we can't always control the way the information is delivered to a new person. If you use a marketplace to sell your work, you can't brand the entire experience to your specifications, so it's important to take the opportunities you have and make them memorable. It may seem like a lot of work to send special notes to all your customers, but it can make the difference between a one-time customer and a devout evangelist.

Customer Expectations

Each person that comes into your world comes with a laundry list of expectations. Sometimes those lists are small and easy to accommodate. Other times, no matter how hard we try, we can't live up to their expectations, but that's ok. We shouldn't try to be all things to all people. If we are being authentic to our business vision, the crowd will sort themselves out.

If you can't live up to the expectations of every customer, you may wonder how are you supposed to tap into that sacred space of knowing how to market to them? (Knowing your ICA backward and forward is a good start.) You learn to create products with that individual in mind. Where there is one person who feels passionate about your brand, there are bound to be many, and if you can tap into them, your message will resonate in an instant. If you, as a customer, have come across a person or company that aligns so perfectly with your point of view that you had to buy from them, then you know what I'm talking about. The goal is to understand your customer's expectations because you understand your customer inside and out.

Service and Support

I shop at a local grocery market where a majority of the employees seem to hate their jobs, maybe even their lives. No matter when I go in, no matter whose line I get into, the people never smile. This store was one of the first to install the self-serve checkout lanes that are becoming more popular, and now I use those lanes more often. The self-serve lanes are not only more convenient, but also allow me to sidestep the sourpuss employees. I want to buy my milk and get on my merry way, but when the cashier scowls at everyone, it makes for an unpleasant experience.

How simple would it be to greet someone with a smile at checkout? Do they have any idea how that simple act would change the mood of nearly everyone they came in contact with. I have tried to use that tactic against them, spreading a cheerful smile to see if I could get them to crack, but with little success. At the end of those visits, I end up regretting going to that store. I would have rather driven to a shop miles away because I know I'll get a better customer experience.

Customer service is a funny thing, so simple to perform, yet very few people do it well anymore. Before I was born, gas stations were called service stations because of the epic service you got when you pulled in. That doesn't happen anymore, but can you imagine opening a service station today; one where anytime someone pulls in for gas, one or two attendants jump out to help you pump the gas, clean the windshield, and check the tires? It sounds nuts, but someone might have a killer idea on their hands if they made that a reality. The concept seems far-fetched now, and that says something about our state of customer awareness.

Treat people with respect, give a smile, go the extra mile to provide quality service to a customer, and they will remember you. Even if they were unhappy with your product, if you treat them with respect and kindness, they may walk away happy. Find a way to turn a disgruntled customer around, and you may have a customer evangelist for life. Customer retention is usually cheaper than finding new ones, so make the best of a situation and provide excellent service from start to finish.

Follow Up

Another simple concept that seems left to the nostalgic days of selling: Someone buys from you, and after, you follow up with them to see how it's going. In the past it was a phone call or letter in the mail. Today it could be an email, tweet, or a post, but the effort of getting back in touch could help foster loyalty.

You may sell dozens of products a day, making it tough to reach out to every customer, but each one gives you an opportunity to consider what you can do after the sale to ensure a return visit or referral? Ask for their email address to get back in touch later, send a postcard in the package that lists your direct email, or post a scheduled tweet that reaches out to them exactly a week or two later to find out how they like the product—a few of many possibilities that require minimal effort, can net big gains.

When you go out to a restaurant, you have a realistic expectation of the times a server will come to your table. They take your order, bring your food, and five to ten minutes later, they check back in to see if you need anything else. They follow that with a suggestion of desert, a to-go box, and then the check. It's a method as old as sales itself, and it works. If they miss out on any of those touchpoints, you start to wonder what happened with the service.

Maintaining a healthy level of communication with your customers, whether expected or unexpected, is one of the best ways to keep a relationship solid. Follow up after a sale, be courteous, provide assistance, and maybe ask for a referral. Open yourself up to opportunity, and they might reward you. How you interact with customers, treat them during the buying process, and answer their questions and concerns all stack up for or against their opinion of you. Keep that bubble on the right side of the line, and they will speak kindly of you. Give them the most powerful buying experience they've ever received, and people will shout your praises from the mountain tops.

AESTHETICS

This may surprise you, but I believe the identity of your brand is far less important than the quality of your work, and the story you tell, because aesthetics are superficial and forced. Logos and pretty pictures are manufactured to make you look pretty, and that can be an illusion if the rest is not handled well. However, I still believe the aesthetics of your products, marketing collateral, packaging, and overall image representation go a long way to establish you as a professional that people should trust.

Think of any large brand that you respect. What is it about their overall look and feel that makes you a believer in their products? Is it the logo? Do the colors create meaning with you? Does the package make you swoon? I doubt any of those are true independent to themselves, but combined, the visual elements of that brand make you stand up and take notice.

Before I became a graphic designer I was a Microsoft Windows guy. My first computer was a Compaq with Windows 3 installed. I'd seen the Macintosh computers some had, but they were so far out of my budget, I didn't think twice about them. Truthfully, back then, the Macs weren't that impressive to me in comparison. Even after I'd become a professional designer, I worked on Macs at my job, but my computer at home was still a Windows machine. I could get the software I needed for the PC, so I didn't need a Mac. Then Steve Jobs went back to Apple

When I started my job at the publishing company, Apple introduced the iMac, with the jellybean colors. It wasn't powerful enough for the work I did, so I wouldn't have bought one, but they caught my attention. Later, Apple introduced the aluminum-case Mac Pro desktop machine. I bought one a few years after they came out, and I never went back to Windows again.

At the time, Apple were the renegades in the computing world. They hadn't taken over the market yet but were on their way. Back then, it was cool to be a crew member of the pirate ship Apple, led by Capt. Jobs, where *Stay Hungry, Stay Foolish* was our chant. We would take a bullet for the man, but not just because it was cool to be part of the cult. Apple spoke to designers because Jobs showed, inside and out, that he respected the tenets of design in everything Apple did. From the machines, peripherals and packaging, to the commercials, magazine ads, and logo stickers that came with every product they sold—Apple is *design first* at every turn. I've been an evangelist for over a decade, but in 2014, I gave up my iPhone for a Samsung.

I will be a customer of Apple's computer systems for years to come, but the need to be part of the cult is dwindling as other companies come in and do to Apple what Apple did to Dell, Blackberry, and Microsoft. The Samsung spoke to me; it's bigger, lighter, and as an aging bugger with dwindling eyesight and fat fingers, the Samsung meets my needs. I still believe in Apple, and their aesthetic is second to none, but their story has changed, and it's no longer perfectly aligned with mine. The design helps, but it only carries the brand so far in my eyes.

Nobody bought a product they didn't know based on a beautifully crafted logo, but if that company has a compelling story, a beautiful logo will make it better. It's important to keep in mind, while aesthetics will help you support a strong identity, they are not the backbone of your brand. The aesthetics should be nice, but you must follow them up with quality products and service.

Photography and Imagery

You may have been told at times during your creative career that quality photography is important. It's not important—it's essential! People are inherently visual, and if they are looking at your product through a web browser they can't use their other senses to help them make a buying decision. The tactile aspects of your product are moot, as are the scents and sounds—their eyes must overcompensate for the rest. In other words, people online are scrutinizing you even more than they would in person.

It's easy to get overwhelmed with all the different skills you can learn as an owner of a small business. You can learn to code to keep up with the demands of your website. You may want improve your writing to make your blog posts more tantalizing. Those may be important skills, but if you ask my opinion, I advise you to learn how to take better photos. A higher-quality image shared across your multiple online platforms will carry more weight than a crappy image. Shooting nice photos, picking a consistent style, and then sharing those photos often can solidify your standing with your fans and followers.

The beauty of taking a good photograph is that you don't need a high-end camera to do it. The mobile device in your pocket can take excellent photos as long as you know its strengths and weaknesses. This requires some study, experimentation, and practice, but I'm seeing pro-level photography come from a mobile phone more often these days. The beauty of it being a mobile device is that you can go on YouTube right now, type in *mobile phone photography how-to*, and have thousands of video resources on taking a better shot that you can apply instantly.

As with photography, the same goes for the graphic imagery you create for your brand. Whether you made a banner to go on your site, or text based quote to post to Instagram, user-created graphics are ubiquitous now. Like photography, though, the majority of people creating DIY graphics have no design reference or background, and it shows. They string together type styles at random because it looks *cute*, but have no frame of reference for what makes an effective graphic. A web app like Canva can help, but these options are still plagued with people thinking they can do whatever they want to the templates. Technically, this is true, but the question of whether they should or not is up for debate.

Again, YouTube can be your friend. A quick search will bring back tons of videos about the ins and outs of graphic design basics. Canva does provide some great live-action tutorials, but try to step outside the box of those tutorials, because plenty of Canva users are using the same templates, and everyone is starting to look alike. If you really want to step up your game, you could check out sites like Skillshare.com, Udeme.com or Lynda.com and get on-demand training toward almost any subject you can imagine. Those are next-level ideas, but maybe what you need is next-level thinking to get you beyond the scope of your competition.

What it comes down to with your aesthetics is making a decision to create a cohesive visual style to your images, whether that's photography or graphics. The more your imagery is aligned with your brand, the better.

Packaging

I had a conversation with The Yellow Loft's Katrina Luong, who specializes in packaging design for corporate clients. Her philosophy with packaging, as a designer, is that she wants to make sure the person opening the package has an intimate and intricate experience with the process. The packaging should open effortlessly, maintain multiple layers, and be a reward and reminder to the individual of the awesome stuff inside. Extra space is unwanted, but too little space can create a cramped feeling when fingering their way through small cardboard flaps.

Packaging is something many small businesses don't put enough thought into. They buy their bags or boxes from a traditional supplier, maybe toss a sticker or a stamp on it, and call it done. Most sellers want the most efficient packaging possible in order to get it to the customer quickly, but rarely do they consider the experience of the user once the package hits their mailbox or front porch. If it's just a matter of tearing open the end of a padded envelope and pouring the contents out onto the table, did you make an impact with your buyers? If you did, it probably wasn't a positive impact. They may love the item they bought from you, but do they love you? Without a strong package design to make the experience memorable, you lost an opportunity to find out for certain.

Logo Marks

As suggested earlier, nobody buys a hamburger because of the golden M on the package. They don't buy shoes for a swoosh, or books because of a penguin on the spine. Yes, people may buy an Audi because the love Audis, but they didn't buy the car because of the four entwined circles on the grill.

As with any imagery, an ugly logo isn't doing you any favors. Logo design is tricky, and a good one will cost you a decent penny, but a strong logo will carry its weight. If you invest in any graphic design for your company, a logo is where you should put that investment first. You might be able to churn something out yourself that is reasonably palatable, but the chance of creating a good, memorable, and timeless logo mark on your own is slim.

There are services where you can buy a logo for as cheap as $5, but it pains me to even say those words. Do not be enticed by this unicorn—you will get what you pay for. In fact, you would be better off cobbling together something on your own, but don't do that either if you can avoid it. If you're looking to create a long-lasting brand, and want a logo that you can build a brand around, then invest money now. Spend a few hundred dollars and get a local designer to help you. You won't regret it later as you grow.

Keep the design simple, effective, and timeless. Don't use

trendy typefaces or colors you'll grow tired of later. Think of the brands you love. Even though a corporate logo may have developed over time, does it look trendy or timeless? Do they swap out colors and patterns often, or do they keep to a standard? Whatever their approach, I guarantee it is by design, and they spend thousands upon thousands of dollars to keep that logo mark timeless and relevant.

Typography

For my own brand, I use a combination of two standard typefaces, and one accent font called Edo. It was a free font that I picked because it was grungy, yet readable. Instead of typing it out and leaving it be, I prefer to manipulate the size, overlap the letters, tighten up the spacing to give an urban, handwritten feel to the words.

Lately, I've noticed more people using the Edo font in their work. It's even a featured typeface in some popular apps that allow you to place words over photos. Part of me thinks it's time to move on to a new accent font because Edo is becoming too common, but then I think about how much energy I put into making that typeface mine. Nobody else is using it like I use it, and even if does show up in places often, when people see my usage, they know that I spent time to make it unique.

Edo won't last me forever; it is a bit trendy, but I never intended it to be permanent. It's an accent to the core fonts I use, the ones that will stick with me for years to come because I chose timeless typefaces that always look strong, edgy, and modern. When I grow tired of Edo, I will find a new way to accent my type, and that will become part of my brand, but I'm not swapping out typefaces on a whim. Every choice is done with thought and care. I know that if I use type to my advantage, I can create an identity that lasts.

Brand Collateral

I was working with a client recently, establishing a plan of action for a relaunch of their product line, and it included a new brand identity on everything they do, right down to changing the name of the company. It's a massive undertaking, and we took the process slow and steady. As we got to the part where designing brand collateral (business cards, post cards, brochures), it occurred to me that in this era, most of the pieces we would design in the past are useless now. I don't know many people that create brochures anymore, unless they're going to a trade show, but even then, all the company's features can be listed on a website. No sense spending money on something that most people will toss in the recycle bin when finished.

Today, that company has exactly two pieces of collateral: a business card, and a small postcard that includes useful information about the product itself. Again, this could be provided on the website, but we decided to add this one as a printed piece just to give a bit of an elegant touch to the packaging when a customer opened the product. It wasn't necessary or required, but since we are repositioning the brand higher in a more luxury market, the goal is to create a perceived value that goes above where the brand was before. Adding collateral elements can give this perceived value, but they need to make sense and not become an afterthought just to put something extra in the box.

If you are set on making new collateral pieces, keep them dead solid on the brand identity. Keep the design universal across everything, don't sway too far from brand colors, and make sure the lineage from one piece to another is congruous. This is not the place to test out new identity ideas.

Now that you have a primer on the fundamentals of branding for creative businesses, it's time for some heavy labor. Having a basic understanding of the above elements gives you the path. Next, we take steps to making big changes in how we develop a memorable brand. Whatever comes next for you, remember that your efforts are meant for the long term. This is not a race to the finish to see who can build a brand the fastest. Speed has its advantages, but focus and attention to quality have a longer shelf life. There are no quick bucks in branding. It's a long, tedious process, but with each step, it gets easier and more fluid.

Recently, I've taken to cooking more often (which makes my wife happy). There's a common process in cooking called *mise en place*, which is French for putting things in place, or in other words, the prep work done before any cooking begins. You portion out the spices, chop the vegetables, and prep the meats so when the cooking begins, you don't waste time with prepping while your sauce burns.

The work we do now and throughout the remainder of this book is the *mise en place* to our brand. We're setting the foundation now in order to make the work throughout the coming year easier. You may be tempted to apply some of what we talk about to your brand right away, but I caution you to get through the whole process first. You might find there are elements further along that help solidify what you learn early on. If you stop this process too early in order to take some action, you may end up doing extra work in the long run. Do that too many times and you will have a bad experience, which might lead to you tossing the whole book out the proverbial window. Lay the ground work now so you can build upon it later. It's time-consuming, but will result in a richer experience in the end.

ARE YOU MY ICA?

When I first heard the concept of ideal customer avatar, I went headlong into the process of creating my own, but I made all the mistakes I'm trying to help you avoid. I followed the directions, wrote down all the dreams and aspirations of my customer, and when I developed my initial ICA, I came up with a character that felt familiar. If there was a possibility of a female version of myself, I definitely found that person in my ICA. When I shared this person with a friend, they reminded me that I wasn't supposed to find myself in the character, so I went back to the drawing board.

The next incarnation came out a considerable distance from myself, and it seemed like I nailed the concept. Without going into laborious detail, they were a creative spirit who had the talent to make a go of a business, but lacked the confidence and, more importantly, lacked the income to invest in their future. Do you see the problem yet?

I shared the new ICA with my friend again, and they came back and asked me the most astounding and appropriate question: How was this person supposed to pay for my services? I didn't have an answer, but I knew that my definition of this person was spot on, because many creatives suffer from a lack of inspiration, a lack of funds, and a need for direction toward greener pastures.

Why couldn't I make this person my ICA? They needed me, or so I thought. I wanted to bring them into the light of their future success. The problem, I soon found out, is that many of those underfinanced, under-inspired souls thrive in their lack of self-reliance. I don't say this to poke at them, but to acknowledge that in any career environment, there will be people who are perfectly OK existing in that world of scarcity. However, it's not a good place to find an ideal customer.

Sometime after, I heard another business person relate the idea that we must focus our energy on the customers we want, which may not be the customers we have. That statement dropped a neutron bomb on my head, and ever since, I've looked at my potential customers in a different way. Now instead of the downtrodden and destitute, I seek out the inspired and ambitious who know the value of investing in themselves.

It's all well and good to chase after altruistic ideas, saving people from themselves, or giving your work away for next to nothing because it made some poor sap happy, but at some point you need money to make a viable business. When picking your ICA, make sure you know the customer you want to serve, more than the customer you currently serve, and make sure that person can afford you.

4

CREATING A BRAND IDENTITY MANIFESTO

Now that you have a basic understanding of the elements, it's time to discuss how to implement them in a concerted effort across the spectrum of a calendar year. By the end, you'll be able to work out a month-to-month, week-to-week plan of action of thoughtful branding, marketing and sales techniques. As you work your way through your calendar, it's important to remember how each element works with the others to create the story you want to share with the world. Before we dig into that calendar, though, there's groundwork to be done.

Back when I worked as a brand and advertising designer, it was common to create a brand identity package for clients looking for an image overhaul. We designed the logo, chose the font combinations, picked color palettes, and gave all of this to the client in a booklet with recommendations on how to keep the identity consistent. We'd show how a logo should be used with images, how everything should be spaced in relation to each other, where variance was warranted, and what deviations they should avoid. The complexity of the document could be anything from a single page of notes, to an entire book filled with examples. Some clients saw these identity guidelines as a frivolous expenditure. We assured them if they didn't use these identity guidelines, they would be leaving the control of the brand to their employees and contractors. This creates a risk of people using the branding in the wrong way, causing confusion in the marketplace.

Later, while working at the publishing company, I recall flipping through one of the magazines we published. While going page to page, one of the blow-in cards (those annoying things that fall out when you're reading the magazine) caught my attention in a bad way. Someone had taken the magazine's logo and filled it with a rainbow gradient instead of the standard white or yellow. The department that did the collateral like blow-in cards worked independent and autonomously from the design staff at the magazine, which I never understood. Deviations like this were common and, to say the least, frustrating. Because of the lack of communication between teams, these problems arose often, but if the marketing department had a brand identity document to reference, those deviations might not happened.

You know your business, and you may not think you need a guidebook to tell you how to use your logo, fonts, and colors, but having a brand identity to rely on in uncertain areas can help guide your branding in a fluid and cohesive way. I recommend this approach, but instead of just having design elements listed in the document, I suggest taking your brand identity to the next level and create a manifesto that incorporates all aspects of how you put yourself out into the world. What if instead of fonts, colors, and logo placement, you had a document that set the tone for how you approached your customers, your blog, your social media, and everything in between?

There will be times when you're trying to figure out what would be the best thing to post in the different social media outlets. If you had a guideline of what you know works best for you in any given situation, those questionable moments would happen less often.

Imagine you are starting a new product line. You create a product, snap a good photo of it, and have an effective, well-written description ready to go. The standard approach for most small business owners is to blanket the world with that item in one fell swoop, sending the same message to every media outlet, but perhaps there is a way to be strategic about those postings.

Your fans and friends interact with you differently from one outlet to another. Doesn't it make sense to share your work differently across those platforms as well? Create a manifesto about your approach to each, and you'll know at a glance how a post should work in Twitter vs. Instagram vs. Tumblr.

BUILDING THE PERFECT WEAPON

The beauty of a brand identity manifesto is that once you write it, the content solidifies itself in your mind. I'm a big fan of Field Notes notebooks, and the company tagline is, *I'm not writing it down to remember it later. I'm writing it down to remember it now.* This is the concept behind the manifesto, and by putting all this information down on paper, we are implanting the ideas in our head for easy recall later. We may not always remember the small details, but the broad-brush ideas will be present in our minds when needed because we took time to be thoughtful and thorough with our branding.

As we break down the elements of what makes up a brand manifesto, keep in mind that this should be a living, breathing document. What you put into your manifesto may differ from year to year, platform to platform, and some of the questions may not have answers until you put these techniques into practice. All elements in this chapter should be considered, but don't feel obligated to fill them all out right away. Write down the main portions and if you know the answers, fill them out, but if you're stuck, leave it for another time. If certain social media platforms confuse you, wait until you understand them better before committing your thoughts to the manifesto.

If you are stuck, be patient and take notes. Each time you're in a social space, make note of what worked for you, and what didn't. Maybe it's post frequency, or times of day that get the most engagement. Maybe the type of post you shared works better—do images get more reach than text? When you see something that worked, write it down and put it into a further examination folder for review. How you go about this discovery isn't as important as the process of trying to understand it. The more you understand what works for your fans, the better you'll be able to make an impact with them in the future. A deeper connection with people means more engagement, which leads to more fan devotion, and more sales.

Manifesto Anatomy 101

To kick this off, let's break down this document into three main sections: design, storytelling, and tech. Design covers all the bases with logos, fonts, colors, images, and how they work together with your words. Storytelling is the way you approach your different media outlets, and how to best use your personality in those spaces. Tech is more about what times to deliver content, how frequent to share, adding a mix of what content goes where.

Not all of these elements may be clear or necessary for you and your brand right now. Some design aspects might be a mystery if you've never dealt with that side of your business directly. If you need help, ask a friend or colleague what they think about the question. If that friend is a designer, even better, but they may want to help you redesign your entire brand, so tread carefully. I've found that even if someone didn't have a complete understanding of a question, the effort of them trying to figure it out can spur new ideas within them.

At this stage, there are no wrong answers. Power through the sections whether you think they make sense or not, and once you have it complete, you can go back and refine. You will hone this content over time as your ideals about your business change. What is correct right now could change tomorrow, so don't get caught up in making things perfect the first time around. Done is better than perfect, always.

Also, how you write this document is up to you, but you should think of it as reference material. Perhaps you will look back at it later to remind yourself of the plan, or you may hand it off to a future employee to help you. It's best to avoid jargon, and to be concise. Get to the point, be deliberate, and give yourself examples often. This is a tool for helping you make the most of your branding effort, and a tool needs to be useful from the moment you pick it up. There's no misunderstanding how to work a hammer when you hold one, and this manifesto should be the same.

DESIGN MANIFESTO

Before we get into the space, I want to acknowledge that there are two types of people reading this section: the cans and the cannots. Some of you may be well equipped to handle your own graphic design, or you have a mild understanding of graphic software. Those people may or may not get value out of this section, but I'm guessing everyone can learn something about their craft.

On the other hand, there are those that do not know the difference between vector and raster. They don't know what a clipping path is, or how kerning works. That is ok, because even if you do not know any of these terms, and you have no desire to do your own graphic work, it's a good idea to know a bit more about the craft so when you do talk to a graphic designer, you can speak their language.

I do not expect anyone to come out of this section understanding all aspects of what makes good design, mostly because I only know so much. Take this info, write down your thoughts about the visual representation of your brand, and then build upon those ideas with the help of your favorite pixel pusher. If that happens to be you, it wouldn't hurt to run this part of your manifesto by another designer friend. Outside perspectives are always useful. You can always join the Fresh Rag Army group on Facebook and pose your questions there to get insight from other creative business owners.

Logo Design

Starting with the cornerstone of brand design, your logo is a launching pad for the rest of your visual identity. The point of the logo is to give a sense of you at a moment's glance. It may not always be possible to convey your work in icon form, but it can kickstart the idea in someone's mind. Combining a great logo with the rest of the elements of your visual identity can tell a good story about who you are without ever saying a word. Unfortunately, the same goes for a crappy logo. You might have a decent website template with beautiful colors, but if your logo looks amateurish, you will have undone all that great website work in an instant because the logo was the first thing a new visitor saw on your page, and it screamed, "I don't care enough to pay for quality design."

Once you have a solid logo design under your belt, consider how that logo is used in a variety of circumstances. What color variations should you allow, how big should it run in comparison to other elements on the page, and what is the spacial relationship of the logo to other things on the page? How you manage this is something you should discuss with your designer, or experiment with in detail if you are the designer, but all should be noted and held to firmly.

Logo Colors

The two areas you need to be clear on with logo colors are variation and implementation. When you have your logo designed, it may be a single-color situation because that is what works with the design. Any designer worth their salt will give you variations to use in different circumstances, but not all designs do well with color variation. When contracting someone to design a logo for you, make sure you ask for a design with color variants that make sense.

For my brand, the colors are simple: gold, black, white, and occasionally shades of gray. For the most part, my logo design is in black, with the gold star that separates the words. However, the three colors are interchangeable depending on the environment they are being used. On black backgrounds, it's gold with white, or vice versa. Gold is my accent color, so I try to use it somewhere in the design always, and then use white or black where needed most. The star in my logo is always a different color than the words, never the same color all the way across. It's these tiny distinctions that clarify the design for others. If I was to hand over the logo to someone else, I would give them the variations needed and ask that they use the images as is. Clearly defining it from the start is how I maintain design integrity.

The second area you need to be clear about your coloration is how those colors are represented in different spectrums, namely RGB, CMYK, and hex. CMYK is the source for color process printing, RGB is how colors are rendered on screen, from computer monitors to televisions, and hex relates to screen colors as they appear on the web, based on a hexadecimal code that gets read by web browsers.

For all of what you do online, hex is the one you'll use most. Knowing the hex codes for your palette will help you make web decisions easier, and will allow people working for you access to specific colors instead of guessing. There are plenty of tools online to help you figure out the hex code, but if you have Photoshop or some other image rendering software, all of these spectrums are built in and easily accessible.

The problem with going from web to print is that sometimes colors don't represent the same when you switch from one to the other. RGB and hex use an artificial light source that can't always be replicated in print. Some bright blues, reds, and greens are impossible to achieve in print, so it's important to understand how your chosen colors for your logo are rendered in CMYK. In fact, I recommend you start with CMYK before moving to RGB or hex. Again, any print designer worth a damn will know this and be able to help you.

Before moving on, let's talk briefly about Pantone colors, which are specialized mixes created by the Pantone company. Most people will never see or need these colors, but let's assume your logo and palette has a bright and brilliant color like fluorescent green or Cerulean blue. These colors cannot be recreated in print using the CMYK process. You can't get to that level of brilliance within the CMYK spectrum, so we turn to Pantone. If you're using these colors, keep in mind that your printed material will be more expensive because of it. If you can avoid them, great, but sometimes you gotta have the exact hue you want. Tiffany blue is a one-of-a-kind Pantone color for a reason. We don't need to go into more detail than that, but if you want to know more, head over to Pantone.com for more color indulgence.

Logo Placement and Size

As mentioned earlier, you'll want to consider size and placement variations of the logo whenever it's being used. Too tight, and the logo is crowded and ignored. Too loose, and it gets lost on the page. The negative space (distance between objects on a page) that surrounds your logo can make all the difference in its impact, and rarely does making the logo bigger have much effect, other than floating your ego, You're better off with math and a good ruler to help you with the proximity of elements on the page.

If you've ever compared a piece of art that was edge to edge against an ornate frame, and then another that had a decent amount of matting between the frame and the work, you know what kind of impact that matte board can give the art. Spatial relationship is important to all aspects of your visual identity, and even more so to your logo.

Using Apple as a benchmark, the logo is almost always white, because that's how it appears on the laptops, and on the devices at startup. Sometimes you might see it in gray, similar to the aluminum of the machines, and only in rare occasions in black only when there is no better option. They also have a very strict size relationship to the page, and the area around the logo is always spacious. Because the color is monochromatic, they want to make sure it's identifiable at a distance, and the best way to manage that is to keep away from other things on the page.

Logo Variations

This subject doesn't get talked about too often in design circles, because it's almost an accepted conclusion that you do not mess with the logo, ever. Although I agree with that sentiment, I believe there may be certain aspects to a brand name that can live beyond the scope of the original logo, and it all comes down to style.

We've all seen brands, often clothing companies, that have an established logo, but they also produce variations on the name itself as one-offs in order to express their style. We assume Nike will always use its name with the swoosh, but there are times when the name Nike is written on clothing in a different typeface, or a swoosh represented a bit looser than normal. It might be a deviation off the actual logo, but if it keeps within the scope of their style. Nike can make these small trips into other areas without damaging the brand, because their brand is so well established. The key is to make the deviation and then get back to home base right away to remind people that the deviation was a temporary thing. The logo will always be the logo, but you may also have some other designs to share, if it makes sense. This does not give all companies carte blanche to change up their logo, and until you're a bit more established,. When in doubt, stick with your primary image.

Typography

Mixing type styles is by far one of the most intricate sciences a graphic designer will ever encounter. It's common practice to have two or more complimentary or contrasting typefaces because it gives depth where one typeface cannot. You grab a serif font (Bodoni), mix it with a sans-serif font (Helvetica), and perhaps the initial combination works great, but before you commit to using the combo, it's smart to test them in multiple scenarios. What works in a logo may not work on the written page. Just because a typeface looks good in a headline/subhead scenario does not mean it will translate over to long-form content. Test and tune as needed. You're going to be with these fonts for a while, so you want to be happy with them.

When you do find a type combination that works, you'll need experimentation with size and space relationships. This takes time and you will always run across new situations where the old rules you've created don't apply. Sometimes what you have dictated as your type style guideline can be challenged by the most random piece of marketing collateral or advertising. What do you do in those situations? The short answer is to improvise and move on, but the long answer is that you can't get caught up in the endless possibilities. You have to move forward. Pick your typefaces, use them as noted, and if a unique problem comes along, find a unique solution.

As far as type style, there are no rules here. You can use any combination of fonts you want, but remember, not all typefaces are created equal. You don't want to use campy or decorative typefaces that will go out of style, at least not as the core typeface of your brand. Papyrus and Comic Sans should not be anywhere close to your radar. If they are, then you need more design help. Put down the mouse and slowly back away from the computer and hire someone to find a better font to use. Sometimes those campy fonts can work, but you need to be aware of the taste level when implementing them. Remember that type is meant to be legible in most scenarios. When you use type, the reader should be able to get into that content without struggle. There are always exceptions to rules like that, but this one stands strong most of the time.

Color Palette

I bring up color palette again because even though you may have established variations in your logo, that doesn't mean they are the only ones you will ever use. Again, my logo is a combination of black, white, and gold, but sometimes you'll see me use colors like dark slate blue, or deep crimson, but usually only as background to enhance the logo itself.

Use your current color palette, but test it against other options, in case you feel like spicing up an image in a different way. If you're thoughtful to the style, you can find ways to make it work, and when you do find colors that work with your logo palette, notate them in the manifesto. Remember to notate the CMYK, RGB, and hex color callouts.

You may also find times when you know a certain color combination doesn't work with your palette, or perhaps it touches a little too closely to what a competitor is doing. In that case, you may want to add an exclusion list of colors to not use with your palette.

Photos and Images

How you portray yourself and your work in images is essential to your brand, and establishing that identity right away will be valuable. You may not nail it right from the start, but if you're working toward a goal because you established a certain standard in the beginning, you will gain credibility and loyalty because of the standards you put on your imagery. Whether you're shooting products, people, or environments, make sure to note the goals you want to achieve with your images, starting with style and mood.

Your style will adapt and change over time, and you may not know what your style is at the beginning. When you see other photos you like, it's good idea to save those to a style board for future reference. Pinterest is great for this, or you could go old school and put together a vision board of clipped images, tacking them together in a style guide montage. When I was designing full-time, I had half a drawer of a file cabinet filled with clipped images that I would pull out and sift through for ideas. I would either scan the images in to use in a design, or just look at them to find inspiration within the mix. With sites like Pinterest and Tumblr, I don't have to take up precious storage space in my cabinet, but I get nostalgic sometimes thinking about all the ephemera I would comb through for inspiration back in those early days.

What's important is that you find the common thread in your inspiration and use that as a guide to shoot your own work. I'm not saying you go and copy other people's work, but rather, steal with style; take what you find and make it your own. When you're looking at an image you like, ask yourself how you can use your work in that way, even if there is a disconnect on the content. Maybe it's the lighting, or the emotion of the piece. Perhaps it's the juxtaposition of the elements, or the exact way a person or thing is framed in the photo. What is it about the typography that gets your attention, or the use of color? How can you use those to establish your style? If you're in the early stages of this process, have fun with it. Play with color, mood, lighting, and composition. Then, when you think you have set idea of what works, put that into your manifesto. Maybe it's with words to describe what you like to see in different situations (products, people, environment), or maybe it's putting all your own successful photos into a vision board of "what works" so you and others can go back and reference it later.

Consistency is the key; using similar styles and techniques to evoke a feeling about your work will give viewers a look into who you are as a person and a business. There are many different ways to take pictures of products, but consider what works best for you particular items. It's not an easy question to answer, and there's the risk of doing things like everyone else. Let's say you make jewelry, and you're tired or taking pictures of your necklaces hanging from driftwood, like so many others do. Maybe while you were looking for inspiration, you saw an photo that showed an interesting way something was hung on a wall, and that inspires you to hang your pieces a different way. Perhaps it's not the display that needs adjusting, but the setting. There's nothing wrong with shooting your stuff on a white background, because it gives the truest sense of your product, but does that create the mood you want? If you're looking to add warmth, or depth, maybe a more natural environment is needed. You could also look at contrasting styles, mixing organic with inorganic, natural with industrial. Whatever that style is, find what works with your brand and own it.

If you want people in your shots, whether it's for your products or just for promotional purposes, what kind of people do you need to use to give a sense of your work? Remember, we're not looking at the people you sell to now, but the ones you'd like to sell to. I have a client who makes hand-painted silk scarves, and she was aiming her work toward mature women, which is fine, but for the future growth of her company, I suggested aiming a bit lower in age group and a financial demographic that wasn't on a fixed income. Instead of using her beautiful, yet mature friends in photos, I suggested using younger models for the purpose of attracting similar types. I'm not saying that only these types of women can buy her scarves, but rather, getting the attention of like-minded women who see themselves in the model pictured. If a potential customer sees a model that doesn't resonate with her in age or demographic, she might turn away. This might seem sexist or ageist, and I won't entirely disagree with that, but as a marketer, I must aim my arrows at someone, because shooting wildly into the air without direction isn't going to win me any marksmen trophies.

Environmental photos (urban, nature, local color) can add a lot of depth to your brand because it shows a side of the places you find interesting. If you live in a rural area and spend your time musing while you walk a nature path; sharing that with people can help them commune with you in spirit. For me, I like to feature things like urban decay, architectural signage, and street art. I post it up, tag it appropriately, and people from all walks of life interact with me based on those images. The images don't define me, but they make up a small portion of who I am. The more photos I take, the more story gets created, and more people resonate with my interests.

You don't have to be a pro photographer to make an impact with people. All it takes to create a story is to be consistent with your work and share things about yourself and your business that make sense to your potential customers and fans. Etsy juggernaut, Julie Astrauckas has a successful business selling cute and snarky cards. Her blog at JulieAnnArt.com is filled with pictures of her work, outfits she wears, her travels, and her daily life. She doesn't have a huge following on Instagram or Facebook, but she sells cards like crazy, and it's because she does a good job of sharing who she is as an individual. Her fans love her funny cards, but they didn't become ravenous because of a greeting card that made them laugh uncomfortably. They became evangelist for her because they feel like they know her, and they share their love for her by buying her cards.

That's design in a nutshell. Do you feel manifested? Actually, you might be in a state of overwhelm with all this information, trying to discern what's important and how to manage it. The point of having a clear idea about your visual identity is that it forges the path for a brand experience that your customers can relate to. The other elements in this manifesto might be tangible to you, but may not be as clear for the viewer. A stunning graphic display cuts through the noise and delivers a viewpoint that people can embrace because it's right there in living color. Use these tips as tools to create a beautiful, visual representation of who you are and what your brand represents. The design manifesto doesn't have to be perfectly crafted from the start, but as you get clearer with all of these elements, the document will take on a life of its own, and before you know it, it's almost creating itself. Ok, that's a bit of a reach, but the more comfortable you get with the graphics, the easier they become to produce, and the easier it is to communicate them to others.

Speaking of communication, in the next section of the manifesto, we talk about putting your words to work; no more proverbial story, but actual story writing, or at least story creating. Mixing the the elements of the design with the story might be tricky at first if you're not familiar with the process, but keep putting one and one together until it makes three, and that's when the alchemy happens, but not before you get your story straight.

STORYTELLING MANIFESTO
For years, I've been telling people they need to share their story, and do so in their most authentic voice possible. It occurred to me that some people take that advice a bit too literal, but I do advise that you go and write your way into the hearts of your constituency.

Telling a story can be words, but it can be images too. It can be video, audio, short form, long form, or whichever way you feel like expressing yourself with your work. Sharing your story is at the core of your brand. Even the little things you say in 140 characters can help define you, in both positive and negative ways. If you share from a place of honesty, the right people will buy into you.

When writing this part of your manifesto, a lot of these elements will blend together, encompassed into the larger part of the story. I'm merely breaking them down into several sections to give a clearer idea of how each one can benefit your brand strategy.

What Is This Style You Speak Of?

The interesting (and unfortunate) thing about defining a style is that there's nothing I can tell you about it that will be perfectly clear. Your style must come from within you. No matter what information I share, I can never tap into your perception of style. It's a nebulous thing, and your style may change over time; I know mine has. If you know yourself well enough to define what you like and don't like about what others are doing, you can define and represent that style to your fans and followers.

The best I can advise is to remain authentic to your beliefs, and share them that way. If it's writing we're talking about, write like you were talking to your best friend. You don't have to share intimate details, and shouldn't if that's not your style, but if you don't mind exposing a little proverbial underbelly, go for it. If you like pretty and quaint things, your style should represent pretty and quaint, but what if you suddenly have a need to rant like a sailor? I know people who can pull off the mix, but will it be incongruous to the brand you've established? If you like the idea of a naughty and nice mix, perhaps you can ramp up over time. The true fans will appreciate you for bringing it real.

Style can also be represented in how you publish your message. If you're not down with blogging, then don't blog. If you prefer to share your style visually, then embrace that. For the sake of the manifesto, you may want to write your intention to share visually instead of through words, but only so you have a clear portrayal of your style, right down to the media options you choose.

If I were writing my style manifesto, I would say that I share encouraging words and helpful tips, mixed with the occasional rant. I focus my energy toward artists and designers, addressing those people more directly than others. I want to lift them up, while occasionally kicking them in the pants if needed. I maintain a punk-rock ideology, a boisterous voice, and tender heart that all work together to create a message that resonates explicitly with the people who appreciate those ideals. I'm not for everyone, and I don't want everyone to be on this trip with me, but if you are in, you're in for the long haul, and I honor that loyalty. I would take a bullet for my fans, and my passion shows that in everything I do. A black t-shirt always helps.

Style is about manifesting the essence of you and your work,

THE IMPECCABLE PORTRAIT OF ARIELE ALASKO

If you're not familiar with Ariele Alaska's work, she is an artist and craftsman who works in wood, making hand-carved kitchen implements and art assemblages. Her studio is based in Brooklyn, New York, but spends considerable time traveling and documenting her adventures. It's that documentation that brought me to talking about her here. Of the many people I follow on Instagram, few know how to weave a consistent story through imagery like Ms. Alasko.

One look at Alasko's Instagram feed and it becomes clear why she has hundreds of thousands of followers. She posts consistently, at least once a day, but more importantly, her message is clear from one image to the next. She maintains a distinct aesthetic to her images that represents the feel of her work. Everything is warm, inviting, and joyful without being cliché. She incorporates her projects nicely between photos of her studio, her environment, and her travels. She has a few different themes that she works with, like holding items with one hand outstretched, people shot at a distance, playful pics of her dog, and of course, the products shot on a consistent background.

I'm sure Ariele has worked her photos down to a science, and it is second nature for her now to post things fast and frequent, but it's obvious she spends a lot of time getting them right. She puts in the effort and it pays off. Often she will make a note on a post that she has a bunch of things going up for sale on a certain day and time. If you want one of those pieces, you better be on your game, because they sell out very quick every single time, and at an average of $300 a piece. That's a bad gig if you can get it.

Of course this didn't happen on her efforts alone. She's a darling of many popular blogs and magazines, and gets massive press coverage, but that came because she produces quality work, and portrays it in beautiful ways that attract the attention of content editors around the world. You may not be able to copy her success, but you can learn from her lesson. Start with a good product, and then tell a strong story, with images and words. Share your work often and make people smile because the love seeing high-quality work portrayed in high-quality ways.

and then sharing that essence in the way the suits you best. The hard part is identifying that style, and it happens over time, but when you nail it, you'll know.

You've Got Thirty Seconds—GO!

The perfect elevator speech is the holy grail of networking. To be able to eloquently and accurately let people know what it is you do in thirty seconds or less is a feat in itself. To do so in a way that the listener understands you, and is inspired by your words—that is where the magic happens.

You might ask why you need an elevator pitch. It sounds like something corporate business slags use, and you would be right. To convey who we are, what we do, and what we believe, in a snippet, is a valuable marketing asset for those moments where you find yourself in a social environment and someone asks you, "So, what do you do?"

Someone once shared with me a formula for creating an elevator pitch that is both effective and potentially awe inspiring. It comes down to three simple questions:

Who do you help?

How do you help?

Why does it matter to the person you're talking to?

Now, if you're an artist or maker, *help* may seem like the wrong word, because your work may not help anyone do anything... or does it? Sure, the 20x24 original painting I bought from an artist may not help me do anything tangible, but when I sit in my lounge, sipping a bourbon cocktail over ice, and I look at the art, it makes me smile. I feel good because, not only did I help an artist by buying their work, but it helps me feel more comfortable in my environment. I feel enriched because I have an original piece of art from someone I know will be famous someday. It also helps me explain the value of art to my son because he sees it in all variations on my wall. It makes my home look nice, and when people see it, they get a sense of who I am by looking at it.

That's how art helps me, as a buyer. Now, think about the items you've bought from others that helped you in intangible yet effective ways. Turn those thoughts around on your own work, then go back and answer the questions above.

The Long Bits

Whether you're blogging, sending out email newsletters, or

posting long-form content on sites like Medium.com, the style of your writing will come over time. A lot of people say they enjoy the way I write, but I can't begin to tell you how, when, or where I established that style. I never made a conscious decision to put the words together the way I do, yet here I am.

If writing is your thing, then rock that thing with all your might. People like words, and they love to hear from people who inspire them. Your work makes people feel good, and if you're sharing your written story at the same time, then they will love you even more. Just make sure you stay true to yourself in your words. Get contrived, or step out of your normal style too often and people will think you're trying too hard. Don't try to be Charles Bukowski when your personal style says John Updike.

The Short Bits

The way you express yourself in long-form should extend into social media. However, it's a lot tougher to be clever and on point in 140 characters than it is in a blog post. Practice makes perfect with all things, and you won't nail it every time, but if you stick to your task of being engaging and entertaining, I think you'll find it easier to post up.

What I do recommend in this part of your manifesto is that you decide which social media outlets are best for you. You may prefer Facebook and Twitter to Pinterest and Tumblr, but you should have small sections of your manifesto dedicated to your approach to each medium. This is especially important if you ever decide to hand over control of your social media accounts to an employee to manage. Not getting a clear message across to them could be harmful to your brand if they are not sharing updates in the way that you would.

Get to The Point, Bill

One final note: Try and be as concise with your thoughts as possible. You don't have a choice with Twitter, but still, do not say with five words what can be said in three. Shakespeare is famed for saying, "Brevity is the soul of wit." In other words, don't be a bore. If you can't keep yourself entertained in this space, how do you plan on entertaining your audience?

TECH MANIFESTO

I once read a blog post from a woman who amassed stacks of

notebooks filled with the dates, times, links, and content from every single social media post she made over the years. In those notebooks, she also had space for notes about the level of engagement of each post. She took social media tracking to a whole new level, and it paid off for her in big ways. This woman, who shall remain nameless (only because I can't recall it for the life of me), grew her following exponentially month after moth because she dedicated herself to knowing when and where her best engagement happened. This is an extreme case, but it is worth noting.

For most of us, we approach our engagement with our fans on a lackadaisical level—nothing tracked, nothing scheduled, and nothing noted, because that takes more energy that we want to spend. However, what you have now that the notebook hoarder did not have, are tools that help you do all the scheduling and tracking of information. Not only can using these tools help you better understand when and where your people are interacting most, but they can make your day a bit easier.

This portion of your manifesto is going to take a bit of research before you start making notes on your approach. You need to have a basic understanding of our people's actions before adjusting the message or how and when it's delivered. For instance, if you have a Facebook page for your business, the insights take provides a lot of information at your disposal. You can find out what posts people connected with most, what times of day you get the most engagement, what percentage of male vs. female followers you have, what is the best age range to target, and where the bulk of your people are located. That's epic information to have at your disposal, and it only takes a moment to see it.

For me, the majority of my Facebook fans are women, the bulk between 25 and 55 years of age; they live near the East or West coast of the U.S. and hang out online between 6am and 6pm. They are on Facebook more on Tuesday, Wednesday, and Thursday, with many pushing their time on Fridays until the afternoon. My highest engagement with fans comes after I share a helpful tip, controversial thought, or snarky and uplifting quotes. I don't have to be a genius to figure out how and when I should be spending my time and energy on Facebook. Add in the capability of scheduling my posts in advance, and I can preload up an entire week of posts in about thirty minutes.

Social Tech

Between blog posts, email newsletters, tweets, and updates, I can schedule my entire social media campaign in the period of half a day, and do so with precision. I use MailChimp as my email autoresponder service. Not only can I set up emails to go out at a certain time or day, but it will calculate based on my previous reader engagement what is the best time of day for me to send on any given day. On top of that, I can write several posts for people to get in a succession once they've signed up for my list, and it's automated so I don't have to do a thing once I write the first message.

Hootsuite allows me to hit several of my social campaigns at once, and I can schedule everything from their user-friendly interface. If I upgrade to their pro version, not only do I get loads of stats to help me better understand my engagement, but I can submit a spreadsheet of information that contains dates, times and content. Hootsuite will turn my spreadsheet into a scheduled campaign that requires little attention from me except to interact with people who have interacted with my prescheduled posts.

Facebook, Twitter, LinkedIn, Pinterest, Youtube, and even your blog give you amazing control and insight to your people, so I advise you take some time to learn how to use these features because they can work in your favor, both in targeting your fans, and also helping you save time online so you can get back to work making cool stuff.

Action Tech

The information for your tech manifesto will be concise and scientific in nature, compared with the storytelling and design sections. The easiest way to build this part of your manifesto is to write down all the social media outlets you use with consistency, seek out some analytics and insight about the who, what, where, and when of your best content in these spaces, and make note about what works best. The *who* is probably the easiest and requires less consideration because we already know who our ideal customer avatar is, if you did your homework from the last chapter.

Write down the best times, days, and content types for each outlet, which should also include your blog and newsletter. Then sit down with a calendar and figure out when would be the best time for you to focus your attention on this. Maybe it's fifteen minutes a day, or a solid few hours once a week, but it's a good idea to block that time to do this work at the same time each day or week, for consistent productivity.

You might want to add some information that talks about the general times and days where your people interact most with you. One person I know uses a grid to show the best times and days for each media outlet as they overlap each other, in a matrix of times and media accounts. For instance, she may have more interaction on Facebook between 7am and 5pm, but her engagement on Pinterest is more like 6am to 3pm, and her Twitter is 10am to 10pm. Given those numbers, it would be in her best interest to schedule the bulk of her posts between 10am and 2pm, because that is when most of her fans engage her during the day.

As with all the elements of this manifesto, it's important to note that the information will morph over time. If you do make changes to any part of this manifesto, keep a copy for reference because you may learn something about the migratory patterns of your people over the course of months or years.

This manifesto concept may seem a bit over the top, and perhaps a daunting undertaking, especially if you're not a professional

Hacking Success with Tech

There's a new term being tossed around the tech world that's shaking up how marketing is performed called Growth Hacking. The term refers to an ideology where the heads of marketing departments in tech companies are no longer MBAs, but engineers. It's been joked that the geeks shall inherit the earth, but it's never been more true than now. No longer will throw ideas at wall and hope one sticks work for corporations. Now marketing must be testable, trackable, and analyzed. If something is not working, not getting the intended return on investment, where is it not working, and how can it be tweaked or fixed?

If you've watched the Superbowl in recent years, no longer are the commercials filled with random tech companies dumping tons of venture capital funding into advertising campaigns that may or may not work. These companies rely on data now, and if there's no data to be found in a marketing approach, or no potential for gathering the data, then it isn't considered. Magazines, radio, and television advertising are dying a slow, painful death because large corporations are getting smart to what works and what doesn't. They want engagement, and they want to be able to track how that engagement happens. Soon, this trend in the tech world will trickle over into the mainstream companies, and big consumer brands like Coke and Budweiser will pull their non-data-driven campaigns for something more tangible, trackable, and testable.

You and I don't have the tools that large corporations have for tracking data, but we have some powerful alternatives at our fingertips, many of them free, and all providing valuable insight into how people interact with our brands. Facebook, Twitter, Google Analytics, Etsy, MailChimp, and others all give you stats about how your interactions hit with people. You have all these robust tools available and you should be using them, because your competition is or will be using them. Soon, these tools will be part of every business' regular routine. Then, getting a leg up will be tougher, but right now you have the advantage.

In Facebook, you can find out when is the best time to post certain content. In Google Analytics, you can track your visitors' path through your site, which pages get the most attention, and how you can alter your site to take advantage of that information. MailChimp not only tells you when is the best time to share your email blasts, but you can segment off the people who open your emails the most. Imagine sending a special email notice to only your most loyal and devoted readers and customers? How valuable would that be to your business?

If you're posting ads in Facebook, you can get super-niche with your approach, narrowing your ideal viewer down to the elements that fit your ICA the best. You can target the fans of your competition directly, and then pick only the ones that fit into your ICA. There isn't a creative director in all of Madison Avenue that has that kind of insight, and Facebook gives it away for free.

The passive approach to marketing is no longer acceptable. You must take an active role in what works and what doesn't. The time of looking at your marketing efforts like an artist is over. Now it's time to break out your inner engineer, learn more about analytics, statistics, customer retention, email open rates, and other metrics that will give you a smarter, more accurate look at what the potential future of your business will be by applying a hacker methodology.

designer or marketer. It may seem indulgent, and you might not see the value of having all this information in a notebook on your bedside table, but if you take the time to put this information together, and add to it over time, you will see a difference in your business. Make a concentrated effort to learn more about your business, and establish rules about what works for your brand. Most small businesses never take this kind of time and energy to properly identify the elements, and we wonder why most businesses fail in the first three years.

Spending time putting this information down into written form not only gives you a resource to reference later, but it solidifies the concepts in your head from the start. Identifying your style, writing down your point of view, and understanding who, what and when to talk to your people will make a massive difference in the engagement you have with your fans and customers. Do the work, or don't do the work, but if you want a bulletproof business that grows day to day, week to week, month to month, that isn't plagued by seasonal lulls, you'll spend some time putting this manifesto together. Think about it this way, the manifesto could be the difference between prosperity and failure, between winning and losing, and if your competition isn't doing this (you can almost guarantee they aren't), then you have a built-in secret weapon, one that helps you capture their fans as soon as they fail. Otherwise, it could be your fans the competition is capturing instead.

This manifesto will help you focus your energy on the branding elements we talk about. Put the time in early, before moving onto other projects, because it may be tougher to go back and do it later. If you jump ahead, you may find yourself deep into these techniques, wishing you had your manifesto handy to reference, or make a quick note about something that shifted or changed.

You know the idiom measure twice, cut once? Yeah, that—all day long!

TIME AS A MARKETING TOOL

Many of the reasons creative businesses languish or fail are because they do not analyze their situation closely. With a bit of forethought, critical thinking, and a strategy on to how to proceed through the coming weeks, months, and years, you can develop an action plan that puts you on a path to success.

Imagine it's the beginning of January (assuming it's not actually January when you read this). You made it through another hectic holiday season. Your shelves are empty, and all your orders went out on time. You survived the family gatherings without anyone going to the emergency ward, and the headaches and soft stomachs of New Year's Day have passed. Now you're motivated to get moving on a new year.

You have your business resolution list tacked to the wall, and you're heading out to the office supply store to get more organizational accessories to make your workspace less chaotic. You want to get a jump on this new year because you're amped over all the sales you made between October and December. Bring on those repeat customers, you say.

You crack open your laptop to check your sales for the day, and hear nothing but crickets. You shrug it off, chalk it up as being too early for buyers, and then go about tidying up the studio instead. The next morning you open your laptop, and you've got a sale! You're ecstatic, and you feel like this year is going to be the best ever, but it's the only sale you get that day. In fact, it may be the only sale you get that week, and for some sellers, the entire month. Welcome to the post-holiday slump of a product-based business.

If you've done creative work for more than a year or two, you know how this goes. The massive crescendo of sales gets you amped about the future of your business, but then the reality of life sets in, and you realize all the shoppers went home. They are shopped out, broke, and not in the mood to buy because they're reeling from credit card interest. In fact, you might be dreading your own credit card bills because of all the gifts you bought, and the supplies you ordered thinking your business would boom in the new year. This year might still turn out to be better than the last, but when does it begin?

If this is your new year reality, rejoice in it, because you now have an opportunity to take stock of what you have going, and figure out how to make changes that benefit your business. Now is the time to start applying all the tricks and techniques you've learned about marketing and apply them to your business. Now we get dirty, implementing strategies that help us build a loyal following throughout the year so when January rolls around, we'll be too busy to worry about cleaning the studio.

We will look at the coming year as a whole, and break it down into monthly, weekly, and daily segments. We'll look more critically at special times of years, and how to approach them. In your first go at this, it may be a massive task, but if you focus your energy, the flow will catch up to you, and it will become easier to think in these timelines.

I recommend you have a calendar handy. Whether that's a physical or digital calendar, that's up to you, but it will become an essential tool. Nothing scheduled = nothing done. Get in the habit of putting every aspect of your business life on your calendar. This isn't about keeping everything scheduled, but solidifying the idea of schedule and organization in your mind to a point that it becomes a positive habit that will improve your business.

For the purpose of keeping to a theme, I use the traditional calendar year as a basis for all the things I talk about, but your seasonal cycles may be different. For instance, a clothing designer ramps up their work for spring and fall collections, which launch in late winter and summer respectively, so it make sense for them to have a different perspective on seasons. Although I speak about the end-of-year holidays as the big push, the concepts still apply to whichever part of the year makes up your busiest times.

The goal is to focus on daily, weekly, and monthly habits to sustain you in the minds of the people paying attention, mixed with strategic pushes throughout the year to boost your promotional awareness in critical times. The key to everything is consistency, which at times might seem laborious and repetitive, but memorable branding is built on the backs of labor-intensive, repetitive consistency.

CALENDAR AS A ROADMAP

The traditional calendar year, as a marketing tool, may not be the same for everyone, but you can still apply these rules based on your own seasonal ups and downs. Don't get caught up the idea that if your'e reading this in February that you have to wait until next year to ramp up. Get started now, and alter the plan as you go. I refer to this plan as a roadmap, but really, it's more a point on the horizon. You have an idea where you're headed, but you will take your own path to get there, instead of following the paths of others.

Before we begin this jaunt through your next year in business, you must start setting yourself up for success, the most important task being goal-setting. You need to establish a goal or milestone that you want to achieve with your progress, because it's easier to hit a target when you know where you're aiming. Perhaps it's that you want to sell twice as many items this year as you did last year, or you want to expand your realm of influence by a certain percentage. Whatever that goal is, write that stuff down. Then post it somewhere you will see if often, to remind yourself what you're working toward.

It's also important to have a sense of purpose behind that goal. Sure, you may want to earn double over last year, but why do you want to double your income? Earning more money is not a purpose, but perhaps it's what that money affords you that defines your purpose. Wanting more fans is not a purpose, but making more fans smile every time they see your work is a good start. Using my own example, my purpose is to help as many creative entrepreneurs get their head out of their proverbial behinds so they can chase a viable, thriving career. My goal is to have at least five to ten thousand more people following my moves over the next year because the more people I can reach, the bigger impact we can all make together. Define your goal, define your purpose, and the rest of it will fall into place. Just make sure you represent authentically.

For the sake of starting at the beginning, let's assume you are starting fresh for the year. You've blown out all your holiday sales, shipped all your product, and now you're continuing on with a new outlook on the coming months with nothing more than an idea and the drive to make that idea happen. Contrary to what some might think, this is a great place to start, because you now have the entire world open to you. You may have a few sales coming in each week, but now we're working to turn those few into dozens, and those dozens into hundreds.

You established your goal, your purpose is set, and it's time to build a plan. You are going to map out daily, weekly, and monthly duties, along with event-based objectives geared around special time periods. How you map this out is entirely up to you, but I would start with a calendar that you know you will look at on a regular basis. Maybe it's a wall calendar, a desktop blotter with big boxes for notes, or a digital calendar, because you can access it anywhere. I recommend the latter, but everyone works differently and it's important to work within your own flow. The important part is to make sure you have plenty of room to write notes about the things you have coming up in the calendar. If you use a physical calendar, consider writing in pencil, because things will change. Being able to erase is a priceless option.

I prefer Google Calendar because I can write different notes in different sub-calendars, giving them each separate colors. At a glance, I can identify what things I am working on that day, and what to prep for the rest of the week. On top of that, I can take it with me anywhere. If you're using a physical calendar, colored pencils are good for identifying separate tasks, or goals. Having that differentiation will help you focus on things just by looking at your day's activities.

The first thing that should go into the calendar are the special events and happenings that will take place only during specific times during the year. Ramping up for the holidays may be one. Back-to-school or tax-time might be others. We start our planning with these events, because during those times, they will become our priority. If you know there's an art/craft show happening in April you want to be in, even if you don't know the dates yet, put that down in the calendar now. If you know you want to take a vacation in summer, mark it down so you can plan around it. It's harder to wedge a vacation into work time than it is to fill vacation time with work, if you end up staying home.

After special events, we move to seasonal items. What things do

I need to do in spring, summer, autumn and winter? St. Patrick's Day and Halloween might not normally be big seasonal pushes for you, but who says you can't indulge? If you're a fan of pagan holidays, why not use it to your advantage, and who says you have to be Irish to celebrate St. Patrick's Day with specials in your shop? My friend Colin is an illustrator who obsessively draws all day long. In October, he participates in *Drawlloween,* where he draws one Halloween-themed picture every day of the month and shares that in his social media with the hashtag #Drawlloween. It may not always have a big impact on sales, but his fan base grows a lot. He can repurpose the illustrations he doesn't sell for another project, or put them up on a stock imagery site, so nothing is a loss. If Halloween isn't your thing, there are plenty of holidays and seasonal happenings that you can participate in, or even create yourself. Maybe you start *Maker Monday* and post something you made on the fly with stuff you had immediately available every Monday for the entire year. There are hundreds if not thousands of trends you can take advantage of to garner more sales and attention. Find something to latch onto or make something up. It doesn't matter, but make sure to mark it down in the calendar so you know to prepare for it.

Monthly events are good for review and reflection time. Maybe you want to check your site analytics for the past month, or take stock of how your fan base has grown. You could map out your editorial calendar, brainstorm a creative project plan, or take supply and product inventory. If you're planning your writing, month-in-review posts where you talk about how the past month went, always score big with people. You can link back to past posts to get people to stick around and read more of your work, maybe eventually clicking your Shop button, and buying something. You could also reverse this idea and talk about what you have planned for the coming month. Posts like these are great for your email list, because it gives an exclusive look at how you operate. You may not think it's interesting, but your fans will dig it.

Weekly dates with your business can be a number of things. Weekly is a good time to share content, whether that's words, audio, or video. In the past, it was de rigueur to blog daily if not multiple times a day, but as the great and mystical Google changes their algorithm, post frequency becomes far less important, taking a back seat to quality content that is on point with the nature of your site.

Weekly scheduling is also good for planning strategy, taking stock of which posts worked, and which didn't, between your different media outlets. If you knew that soapbox rants worked better during the middle of the week, and list-based posts were best on the weekends, you schedule accordingly and follow suit with the social media.

Uploading new work to your selling platform can be on the weekly list, or at least reviewing the items you have in your shop currently. Is there a piece or two that's not selling? Maybe it needs an SEO review of the tags and descriptions. You could review your product photos and set aside time each week to replace certain images that better represent your brand.

My biggest daily work habit these days is writing. I put aside time each day just for putting hands on the keyboard. Getting this book out, and then getting right to work on the next one is time-consuming work, so I need to schedule in the time in order to be as productive as possible. If you find yourself growing detached from the creative work, because you're caught up in other business, then perhaps scheduling in time for creativity will help you get back some of the energy you've spent.

I'm not as good at this as I should be, but I try and schedule social media time during each day. Ideally, I would spend thirty minutes in the morning, and thirty in the evening, just to work on social media. I'd schedule posts on Twitter and Facebook, and set up some images to share on Instagram. The goal is to get in, get work accomplished there, and then get the heck out. When I first started working on my business, I found myself hanging out in Facebook for hours, justifying my time because I was "networking" with people. That's a load of crap, and now I know it. Yes, I can meet people, make connections, but it's definitely not something I need to spend hours on each day. I'm sure you already know how much of a time suck social media can be if you let it.

I spend a considerable amount of time thinking of ways to market myself. Maybe it's creating graphics to share that relate to one of my offerings. It could be ideas on ways to promote and share in places I normally don't touch. I try to not let the marketing ideas consume me, though. I could spend all day thinking of things I could be doing on various outlets, but it's not always the best use of my time. Yes, I could potentially make more money, but at some point people are going to want my next, new thing, and if I spend my time marketing and socializing, I won't be working on that next, new thing. Then I end up with a legion of disappointed people who want what I'm not delivering.

Whichever way you go about organizing your calendar, it's

important to remember to not get down on yourself if you fall off track. Just pick yourself up and get back on it. The approach of special > seasonal > monthly > weekly> daily will reap you benefits if you attack it, and the more you stay focused, the better the return, as long as you're always working toward your goals. Don't get caught up needing to stick to the calendar without fail. I advise using pencil because life will always find away to monkey with your plans, and that's ok. Deal with stuff as it comes at you, handle it quick, and then get back on schedule.

THE ANNUAL REVIEW

As you go through this process, you'll want to start with a big-picture perspective of the whole year in front of you. From there, you'll niche down to seasons, months, weeks, and daily routines, mixing in special events. Before you go there, though, take a look at where your business has been over the past twelve months. Reviewing the past year can lend insight to help shape the coming year, and I'm certain there are plenty of lessons you learned that you can incorporate now to avoid making similar mistakes in the future.

When you sit down to take stock of the past year, look back with a critical eye. Within the past twelve months, there have been clues to what worked well and what didn't, and the only way to know what had a big impact is to take a deep dive into the past. With a notebook at hand, think back to what moments stand out to you in regards to your business. Were there distinct points in the past year where you either saw a big win, or stumbled on a big obstacle? Can you track your ups and downs to certain experiences or times of year?

- Did you participate in shows that didn't work?
- Did you see unexpected peaks in sales during times that you can pin to certain events?
- Are there dry moments where you knew you could have done more promotion?
- Did certain new relationships with other sellers bring opportunity during the year?
- Was your effort on some online platforms more fruitful than others?

By doing a thorough review of the past year and asking yourself tough questions, not only do you give yourself insight on how to approach the coming year, but you also set a precedent for awareness. By looking back at your past, you are opening your eyes to the future. When reoccurring circumstances show their face, you'll recognize them and have a strategy for hurdling obstacles and taking advantage of opportunities.

We don't dwell on the past, and the point of this exercise is not to overanalyze problems that occurred, but to, reflect and learn from those moments in order to create opportunities from them. If you can pinpoint dates and times where substantial things happened, both positive and negative, then those should be noted in your future calendar. For more nebulous moments, where you can't pinpoint them on a dateline, but know you need to act on them when they happen, find a way to add them into your routine.

I stress looking backward because if you don't learn from your mistakes, you will be doomed to repeat them, and when you do that a few times too often, it weighs on your mind, stealing your motivation, until you end up either changing your actions, or giving up altogether. I don't want that any more than you, so a little preventive maintenance now will set yourself up for future success.

THE YEAR AHEAD

Now that you've taken a good look at the past, made notes of times and dates that might have an impact on your future sales, it's time to focus on the coming year. We'll start by looking at the big picture, defining the significant moments, and breaking apart tasks into smaller, ritualistic goals.

As you review your annual calendar, you will remind yourself of things you should be doing on a scheduled basis. On that handy notepad of yours, make sure you have sections for seasonal, monthly, weekly, and daily tasks and projects. As tasks come to mind, and you know where they fit in your routine, mark them down. Work in pencil, and leave room for edits and updates. Change happens, and erasers are gold.

Yearly Times and Tasks to Consider
- Seasonal starts and stops (Christmas, Fashion Week, Valentine's)
- When to bring on physical help (friends, family, indentured servants)
- When to bring on promotional help (ask for pimp skill from the network)

- Holidays that need attention, or awareness (see above)
- Quasi-holidays where you can create opportunities (talk like a pirate much)
- Time off! (yes, this is important)

When you look at your coming year, make note of when your peak seasons start and end. When do you ramp up for the winter holiday, and when does that fall off for you? Consider what would be the best use of your time during these seasons. More specifically, think about what can be done to ramp up earlier in anticipation, and what can be done before the bottom drops out to maintain momentum.

One thing many people don't consider is helping hands. Perhaps there are times when you might consider bringing in part-time help to boost you through busy periods so you can focus your energy on the parts of your business that need your specific attention. Give the more machine-like tasks to someone else. Plan ahead for this, and reach out to people early on, letting them know you'd love their help in the future.

I recently had a conversation with a maker who said that her holiday sales continue deep into January, but February and March were dry for her. She takes that time to build up her inventory for when sales start again. This is a valid option, because you need to have time to make stuff again, but what if she grew her business to a point where she didn't have that dry spell, and she could be selling the entire time? Perhaps she would make enough money to hire a person to help her with aspects of her business (packaging, shipping, administrative), while she continued to handle creation of products as well as promotion? If you want to play in the sandbox with the big kids, it's time to start considering the opportunities to grow your business. We'll dig more into outsourcing later on, but it's an idea I want to plant now because it's important to imagine early, when you don't need it, instead of after it's too late.

Speaking of helping hands, now is a good time to consider where you need to do bigger promotional pushes, whether it's to boost you higher during busy times, or send a message to folks during quieter times to refresh their memory. Can you elicit the help of colleagues to assist you during those times? Maybe it's sending tweets out at certain times in concert with each other to make a big impact all at once, or it's an agreement to share mutual posts on a regular basis. Having partnerships like this will help you in the long term, as long as both sides reciprocate in kind. With a little effort, you can build a routine of promotion from more sites than just your own.

During the year, you know there are going to be holidays that you should take advantage of if you're not already. People who create gifts of love and adoration are already in the habit of focusing on the Hallmark holidays like Valentine's, Mother's Day, and Father's Day, but do you have a plan for reaching out to customers regarding their personal holidays. What if you encouraged people to do more with Facebook birthday announcements than sending a generic and impersonal Happy Birthday message to family and friends?

Again, we're not trying to exhaust ourselves with tasks, but rather, build up a manageable plan that keeps you moving with steady momentum. By putting all these items on a calendar, you are creating a new lifestyle for yourself, one that puts your energy into the business in a more focused way. I don't say this to imply your life should be nothing but business. On the contrary, once you start working a system where all your parts are organized on a timeline, you will find that you have more time for the non-business parts of your life because you set aside time for them as well. These are as important to your success as the business tasks, and at times, more beneficial.

SEASONAL AND HOLIDAY EVENTS

When you think of the annual seasons, consider if there are times you can use to your advantage? For instance, a bikini designer wants to promote for spring, but do they think about the *other* spring? While it may be cold and dreary here in January, if you have customers in Australia or South America, they are in there warm season, so why not promote to them? Another option would be to promote a *pray for sunshine* event in autumn by giving good deals on past collections of your summer items. It's easy to think within the confines of traditional seasons, but the unconventional approach could bring you awareness at a critical moment, when people least expect it.

Can you promote your work as special gifts for birthdays, anniversaries, retirement, or other events that people share within their group? If so, how often might you promote those ideas? These events are happening to someone every single day of the year, so why not add them into your regular promotional schedule in some way?

There's also a chance to invent times to promote, what I refer to as quasi-holidays, where you create a new opportunity to sell. There are national days for just about anything these days. When I was doing research for this section it was National Oatmeal Day. If you sell baked goods, perhaps you could do a promotion based around your tasty oatmeal cookies. The day before that was National Chocolate Day, a date any chocolatier should have on the tasks calendar every year without fail.

When I sold my digital collage art, I always celebrated my birthday and anniversary with special offers for customers. Back then, I wasn't managing an email list (not good), but if I had been, I would have promoted the heck out of those events weeks prior so people could take advantage. Perhaps you declare it your birthday month and anyone who buys in that time, gets a discount. With quasi-holidays, there is really no limit to the opportunities. The point is to have fun with it, and give people an opportunity to share in the fun.

You don't want to do these events too often, because it could become a gimmick, and customers will grow immune. However, if you plan in a few times a year to make a big deal with an uncommon event, you might find a tribe of people looking forward to your annual offerings. The limit to these opportunities goes as far as your imagination, and the more imaginative, the better.

MONTHLY PRACTICES

Along with the more extensive annual review, I recommend doing a monthly preview of events to come. It's best to look at these a bit early, perhaps a month or two in advance, to keep ahead of the timeline so you can produce the work on schedule. If you wait for February 1st to plan for Valentine's Day, you're too late. Halloween should be planned in August, Thanksgiving in September, and Christmas in October (but really, August).

When you look back at your previous year, you might find on average that people spent more money with you in different parts of the month, the 1st and 15th perhaps. You could plan your monthly promotion around these times to take advantage of the influx of money people have to spend, but again, start early so customers know who to spend their money on in advance. First of the month is a tight time for many, and maybe it's weak in sales for you, but maybe use that to your advantage in some fun way—a Blow of Your Mortgage Sale is not necessarily responsible, but it is funny.

I already spoke of my friend Colin who does monthly challenges to illustrate daily in October for the Drawlloween event, but what if he added other times of the year, even if it was only himself. Imagine in December it's twenty-five days of Drawliday Cheer, or July could be InDrawPendence Week. All he needs is an active imagination and a willingness to make it happen.

By knowing your month in advance, you can plan out the conversations you want to have with your people. If you're blogging and writing email newsletters, planning those posts in advance will help make the process smoother. Also, if you know what you are going to write about in advance, you can tease your readers with that information. Tease it well enough, and they'll salivate in anticipation. Take an extra step and create visuals for future subjects, like a famous quote that embodies the subject. Maybe one of your own epiphanic moments becomes the rally cry for a misunderstood subculture.

What started out as random thoughts by a stoner with a flair for inspiration, The Good Vibe is now the number one blog on Tumblr dedicated to typographical, inspirational quotes. Originally titled Kush and Wizdom, the quotes have a young, urban appeal, and quickly became viral because the quotes spoke directly to Tumblr's core demographic: young, angsty teens disenfranchised with the world they were brought into. The simple and original quotes pushed out on a regular basis spread quickly, and before K&W knew what hit them, two million followers were tracking their posts. Recognizing the power of their work, and immaturity of their name, they changed their brand to The Good Vibe to focus on the positivity, and push the marijuana aside. What started as a blog to toke up and get inspired by now has advertising revenue, and they sell shirts emblazoned with some of their more popular phrases. When they started *K&W*, I doubt the blog owner ever expected it to become as popular as it has, but they saw the opportunity to make something bigger, and they took it. This does not mean you should go out and start a Tumblr blog featuring quotes mixed with your vice of choice. Not everyone is good with crafting inspiration, but you don't have to be. If you're not big on writing, you can still create visual elements to embody a theme or event. Quality visuals work well almost anywhere, and will get shared regularly.

One oft-overlooked group is your past customers. You should

pay them special attention, because rewarding them will more likely bring you sales or referrals in the future. It doesn't have to be every month, but a few times a year, make a point of sharing something special as a sign of appreciation. As it's exclusive, it doesn't have to be big to make an impact. Find the monthly rituals that resonate with your fans, represent your products well, and keep people in anticipation of what comes each month.

WEEKLY RITUALS

As you move deeper into the calendar, into items that require your weekly and daily attention, you may find your to-do list becomes massive—perhaps unmanageable. It's easy to get caught up in all the tasks revolving around your business: marketing, packaging, shipping, accounting, and other miscellaneous operations. Believe me when I say that scheduling even the most mundane tasks into your calendar will not only make your life simpler, but you'll get better at it, and your business will run smoother.

When I first pursued my dream of entrepreneurship, I didn't have much of a plan. I relished the cavalier nature of how it all progressed, but as my task list grew, I knew I would be in trouble soon if I didn't get it in check. When I learned to schedule as much of my daily life as possible, it opened up an entire world of opportunity. As crazy as it may sound, blocking out "gym time" in my calendar every day makes it easier to consider what I can do with the rest of my day. I know I want to go to the gym, and I am the one who has to get myself there, but committing to that idea in my calendar makes it more real and keeps me on track. The same goes for any other tasks I have throughout my day. A certain amount of time is dedicated to all the major elements of my business, and I parse up those time slots with micro-goals to achieve during the slotted time.

If I get to the end of a time slot and I need to move on, then I move on. I'm OK with moving on because I know I can go back to that task again later if my other obligations get handled, or it's rescheduled for the next day. The question remains, what warrants a mark in the calendar when talking about weekly and daily tasks? There are some I'm sure you already incorporate, like manage orders, buy supplies, ship items. However, from a branding and promotion standpoint, keeping notes of weekly tasks can improve your marketing productivity. Spend one day a week interacting with customers who have ordered from you over the past week. You could dedicate it to acknowledging customers and their orders, giving thanks for their patronage. You might address concerns, answer questions, or deal with customer service issues. These service items should be dealt with promptly, of course, but you could put a note in your policies that says you address most general questions once or twice a week, to provide a realistic expectation about when most responses will come.

Weekly is also a good time to check simple analytics. Did your Facebook page go up in popularity a lot in a given week? Maybe craft a special message acknowledging the new fans. Perhaps use one day a week to go into Pinterest and be proactive with comments and thank people who have shared your pins. Social media is about being active and social (imagine that), but not all tasks need to be dealt with daily, and you don't want to get stuck in the social vortex of productivity destruction.

One thing I like to do on a weekly basis, if not a few times a week, is pose a question to my fan base in different media outlets. I reserve these questions for Facebook, Google+, and my email newsletter because I know I will get residual attention after a few others have answered. Twitter is tough because of how quick those tweets disappear, but I'm playing with the idea in Instagram with mixed results. More experimentation is needed, but it seems to be a great way to connect and get valuable insight at the same time.

Speaking of newsletters, I advocate interacting with your newsletter readers on a weekly basis, and some sellers opt for bi-weekly to keep from overwhelming readers with emails intrusion. I think that's a fair distance, but don't go further out than monthly. Consistency is valuable and expected. If you disappear for too long, and then come back, people will wonder what happened to you. If you suddenly pop up again, they might lose interest and unsubscribe.

Other weekly ideas should include posting new items for sale, sharing your process, addressing holidays and events in the coming week, touching base with suppliers, and giving random shout-outs to fans for no other reason except to say thank you. It's the little things that count for the most with people, and a small effort goes a long way.

Even if you're not, by the time you've gone through this process, some of those items will reveal themselves. Answering email and interacting on social media should be on your daily tasks, but I encourage putting a time limit on yourself for these things. Items I like to schedule into my daily tasks are time to create, and time for myself. To avoid clutter, I don't put these in the calendar, but the time is there. I know at a certain time of day, I put work on hold so I can hang out with my family. Later, when the boy goes to bed, it's either chill time with the wife, or back to work. Of course, the best gauge is always the look on my wife's face. A grimace definitely means *put the laptop away, Dave.*

THE BIG BIG PICTURE

I'm not a fan of doing five- and ten-year business plans because of the speed at which business moves these days. The work I did a two years ago is far different than what I am doing now, and the work I did five years ago is ancient history. However, there is some benefit to looking further down the road at your business, if only to give you a point on the horizon to aim for while you work.

Looking down the road goes back to identifying your purpose. Purpose can also change over time, but if you can identify the *why* in your business, then looking down that road can be beneficial. For my business, my purpose is to eliminate the starving artist mindset everywhere, and to educate creative people all over the world that their work is valid and important. When I look at that purpose, I can identify where I see myself in five or ten years out. I know there will be a lot more books in my future, for certain. Either my podcast will be more popular, or I will have moved onto a new show that better represents my brand. I also see myself on stage, talking to thousands of people at a time. Having more books, a prominent podcast, and talking to more people is more than just an ego stroke for me. It's about reaching out to more creative people because I have created a world of influence that affects change in others. The more people I reach, the closer I am to achieving my purpose.

If you know the *why* behind what you do, then looking out five years down the road will make more sense, and it will give you the motivation to achieve your goals. Look ahead, and when you see your future, write it down, or post it up somewhere you will see it often to remind you of where you are aiming. If you're just posting grandiose ideas without purpose behind them, you won't find the path to get there, and they will exist only as a dream. Dreams are good, but only when you have a plan to make them happen, and that plan starts with purpose.

STAYING ON SCHEDULE

I cannot stress enough the importance of having that calendar at your disposal. If you use it with diligence, it will change the way you work and, with that, will make you more productive and successful. Of course, just having the calendar isn't enough. You need to put it into action, and then make those actions happen. To achieve a constant flow of business week to week, month to month, year to year, you will need a calendar to know where you stand.

In the past year, I incorporated a piece of cloud-based software that has changed my scheduling life, and it bears sharing. Not everyone agrees with me on this approach, but I see it becoming part of everyone's daily routine in the future. There are many options available, but the service I use is Schedule Once, and its main purpose is to make scheduling time with others more manageable.

In the past, if I wanted to schedule someone for an interview on my show, or give someone a few minutes of my time on a phone call, we needed to do this ridiculous back and forth through email exchanges trying to figure out what times worked for both parties. Now, with Schedule Once, I can set up my available hours for certain categorized tasks, and then coordinate it with my online calendar, be that Outlook, iCal, or Google Calendar. Then when someone wants to schedule something, all I do is hand them a link, and that takes them through a short process where they can find a time slot in my open schedule.

Some people find these services to be business cliché, or self-important, but it has been a lifesaver for me. I can't tell you how many times I have missed appointments because we talked about them in an email exchange, but I forgot to jump over to my calendar to set the appointment. Now there are no slip-ups unless I decide to ignore my calendar entirely.

I endorse Schedule Once as my choice, but there are many options available, and if you do find yourself having trouble keeping appointment schedules straight, I recommend you use one of them to help you out.

FIND YOUR FLOW

There is no one right way to handle your calendar. The information in this chapter is based on what works for me, and what some others use, but it may not work for you. There are many ways to maintain productivity, depending on your attention span and organizational needs. *Just Three Things* works great for me, but it may be too loose for others. If so, check out *Making Ideas Happen* by Scott Belsky or *Getting Things Done* by David Allen. Each of those will give you more productivity tips than you can carry in a pocket notebook.

The structure and organization of schedule management is not about doing things my way, Belsky's way, or Allen's way, but your way. Bringing in new ideas will help you develop a system that can work for you. Keeping an open mind to new ideas will help you build a better method. I want you to find your flow with the calendar, because the goal is to give you more time to do the things you want. The same goes for all the promotional planning. Be kind to yourself on your efforts at first. Don't try to tackle everything at once. Add little bits at a time and incorporate others as you get more comfortable. Your brand is built over time, through trust and authenticity. Be OK with your process now, and improve as you go. You're operating for the long term, not the immediate return. Continue being you, just a little better than you were before.

A TALE OF TWO NOTEBOOKS

For years, I tried to find the perfect system for getting things done, reading many books and blog posts on the subject, but with limited success. It wasn't until I discovered the Moleskine pocket-size notebook that I finally devised a system that works for me. However, my story begins not with one notebook, but with two.

One notebook was my daily carrier where I wrote my random ideas and to-dos. I find it a good idea to write things down when I think of them, because I am human, and am prone to moments of dementia. However, that notebook is a bit of a random mess, and sometimes difficult to decipher what I was thinking.

I started carrying a second notebook to combat the mind clutter of the first book. With the second book, I incorporated a strategy I *call Just Three Things*. Instead of the second book being a catch-all for ideas, it has a very specific purpose: keeping my butt in check. It's not just a notebook, but an entire process to keep me as productive as possible.

The idea behind the process is to give myself three things to do each day. If I accomplish those three things, I can feel good about my productivity. If I finish early, awesome; move on to another task. If I don't finish, I shrug it off and challenge myself to do better tomorrow.

Before the notebook, I gave myself these three tasks, usually written on a sticky note on my laptop, or posted on the wall in my workspace. More often than not, the sticky note on the laptop would get annoying and I would toss it aside. The one on my workspace would go unnoticed if I was working in a different part of the house, or offsite. *Just Three Things* was a solid idea, but lacked proper execution, and I eventually let the concept slide into obscurity.

Finally, after months of being perturbed at my own lack of consistent productivity, I took some time to think about how to incorporate *Just Three Things* back into my life. I decided to use a second notebook, because I knew how important Notebook #1 was to me. If I managed the second book correctly, it could be just as valuable, if not more. When I get ready for my day, I put all my belongings into my pocket or bag. My notebooks are right there to remind me of the tasks I need to accomplish.

The process is simple—I start a page with the day's date, do a quick internal assessment about what my priorities are for the day, and when I figure out which things are most important, I write them into the day's list. The top three tasks for the day get input in sequence from most pressing to least essential. Sometimes this changes after the fact, but at least I've given myself some prioritization to get started.

I try to be specific with my goals because broad goals require too many steps and take too much time. "Finish website" is far too broad and expansive, but "Write sales copy, fix navigation menu, and update sidebar," can be three tasks toward the larger goal. That is plenty to feel productive for one day.

Sometimes, if I feel the three things are easy to achieve, I will add tasks to the list, but with asterisks (*) because those tasks should not be considered before the others— prioritization takes precedence over spontaneity.

Sometimes, when I'm working through my day, a more

pressing issue I forgot about needs to be handled, but didn't make it into the notebook. I ask myself if that task can be handled tomorrow, or does it need to be done today without fail. If it must be done that day, then I do it, but I get my butt back on the list as soon as possible. If it can wait, then I start a new page of *Just Three Things* for the following day, putting that task as top priority.

When I started using the Just Three Things process, I felt there was a piece missing. I often found myself wanting to write down additional tasks that popped up throughout the day, but didn't want to add them to my current list for the day—that would defeat the purpose.

I thought back to something I read in Scott Belsky's book, Making Ideas Happen. In there, He talks about his process of Action Plans, which is an effective idea, but far too intensive for a logically-hindered mind like mine. However, there was one aspect to Belsky's plan that made sense to me.

In the past, I would put the random to-dos or tasks into Notebook #1, but then I needed to muster the motivation to go back there to find the notes. Instead, using Belsky's method, I now write my future ideas into the back page of the notebook. This puts them out of the way of the daily tasks, but still close by to reference when I need them.

Each day, as I take stock of what I need to accomplish, I'll glance back at this list to see if anything on it is more pressing than what I'm currently working on. If so, it gets transferred to the daily list, or perhaps broken down into smaller tasks for the next day or so.

There isn't more to it than that. Find three things to do each day, write them down in something you can carry with you, and then repeat that process every day. When you get tasks done, be happy. When you don't, be OK with that because you can try again tomorrow. Even if you only do one of the three things, at least you accomplished something that day.

It will take time to get into a rhythm, but once you do, you'll crave the opportunity to put three things on your list each day because you'll want to do everything you can to make those three things happen.

Now I can cross this task off my list.

6

··············

BEST PRACTICES

Whether you're brand new to the chasm between seasons, or a long-term veteran, the fact that you're in the slump should make you take notice. If you're in a sales hole, the truth is there are things you have not done to make your business more sustainable. Don't fret and don't dwell—you are not alone. Instead of bemoaning what we did or didn't do to get us in a slump, we must figure out how to fix it, starting today.

Taking into consideration everything you've read up to this moment, the first thing to do is take stock of your current branding and promotional efforts. Assess the holes in your game that you skipped over in the past, and think about where to focus your energy to promote your business in an organic way without coming off like a shill? What can you do with your imagery that will elevate the appeal of your brand? Think about where your biggest growth came from in the past year, and how to capitalize on that growth.

Full disclosure, I am not fond of the term *best practices* because it represents following standards set aside by an old guard that has since been forgotten by time. Many business *best practices* five years ago have become staid and irrelevant compared with how things are done today, but there is still some truth to many of them. When reviewing the following ideas, remember to relate them to your business and your brand before you incorporate them. Not everything said here will work the same for all companies or people, but I'm sure you will find wisdom worth integrating into your life.

The following pages include snippets of information I have pulled together from many areas of my process that I believe can help you make room for more success in your creative business and life. Some of these are interwoven with each other, and others are disparate, but they all work as part of the big picture that is your brand and your business, starting with the most important factor of all: Sales!

MINE YOUR GOLD

When I started writing this book, I had a big problem. I knew that my site's opt-in box was broken. The reason I hadn't fixed it yet is that I made a deal with myself that I would make this book a priority above all other things. That doesn't mean I didn't cringe every day that went by without gathering new email subscribers. It killed me to not fix the problem, but the writing came first. Once this book was done, I fixed the opt-in problem, and the leads started flowing again, which makes me happy. Why would a functional email list make me happy? Because I know its true value.

Since you're ready to take your branding a step above, and the first priority should be your email list. If you haven't established an email list yet, you need to get yourself over to MailChimp, Aweber, or one of the other email autoresponder services pronto! I cannot stress this enough; you are doing your business a disservice by not collecting and maintaining an active email list.

If you have a list, and you're standing at the beginning of our annual assessment, now is the time to reach out to that list. If you haven't touched base in a while, it's a good time to get reacquainted. Send out a thoughtful note right away thanking them for being loyal customers and fans, and tell them you hope for them to have a fantastic new year. This note is not about pitching, but instead, trying to gather feedback. We're aiming for data collection more than anything else, and any feedback or interaction is a good at this point. If you want to get more personal with them, ask them about their holiday, their New Year resolutions, or what they wish Santa would have brought them. If they did buy from you, ask what they thought of the work, and the buying experience. See if you can gain insight about your products or service that you can change or improve upon. If you dropped the ball with a customer, there's no time like now to eat crow and find a way to avoid those situations in the future. You can't please everyone all of the time, but you may find ways to make more people happy, more often.

After you've touched base with your current list, reach out to your social networks, share that you have a newsletter list, and ask them to join. Let them know, now that the holidays are past, you'll be focusing your energy on the newsletter more often. If you ask people to join your list, make sure they know exactly what you're offering them for being on the list. Did you give something away to attract readers? Are you sharing tips and techniques in the emails that they won't find anywhere else? Do they get special shop discounts or exclusives for being subscribers? Before they join, they will want to know the benefit for giving away their precious email address. Figure out your offering, be clear about it on your site, and then share the news about the newsletter to your network.

Some believe email is not the way to go with marketing. Not long ago, someone on Twitter challenged my thoughts on the effectiveness of setting up an email list. They felt email was dying and nobody wanted to be contacted that way anymore. People are tired of spam, so why should we want to make it worse?

My response is that not all emails are created equal, and even the most jaded email user still gets a little excited when certain emails come into their inboxes from people or brands they adore. If all you're doing with your email list is pitching them your latest sales items, then I can see why someone might not want the barrage of messages clogging their inbox. However, if you're providing value, knowledge, and entertainment with your email updates, a percentage of your fans will voraciously consume whatever it is you have to share.

Over my life as an entrepreneur, I've heard many top business experts speak on the subject of marketing. These experts are often asked about the biggest mistake they made in business. More times than not, they say the same thing: they wish they had started their email list sooner. Do not play down this valuable asset, please. Prioritize starting and maintaining your list right away.

A popular phrase in the marketing world is, *the money is in the list*, which is both an accurate and creepy way to look at the people on your list. Of all your online networks, the people on your list are the ones who will buy from you first, but instead of treating them like a dollar sign, I consider my list more of a precious metal. I turned the statement into, *the gold is in the list*, which has a much more potent connotation.

My list is golden because the people on it are valuable beyond any dollars they spend with me. They are the most engaged, most emphatic, most likely to answer my questions when I have them. If I need feedback, the people on my list are the first to answer. If I need to know what my readers like or dislike about my offerings, the people on my list are always the ones to give me the most thoughtful and thorough responses. They may be the first to market when I launch new products, and I respect that instead of taking it for granted. That is why I offer my best discounts, and early bird specials, to the people on my list first.

Your list should be a preoccupation throughout the year, and you should be touching base with them on a regular basis, but for the sake of getting back into the game, start with asking, "What can I do for you? How can I help? What would you like to see in the future?" Some sellers think email is an intrusion, but my experience has shown that my true fans, the ones who want to be on my list, love the opportunities to interact with me. I've built up camaraderie with them, and they know when they write to me, they will always get right into my inbox.

You don't have a crystal ball to tell the future of your business, but being able to reach out to your list is the next best thing, because your customers will tell you exactly how you can help serve them with more products in the future. You don't need to be as available as I am for my readers, but if you ask for input from your list, they will give you what you need.

WHAT DO I WRITE ABOUT?

This is the single most popular question I get from people about starting an email newsletter, hands down, and what it's taught me is to not take for granted my ability to string together a thousands-plus words for the purpose of teaching someone something. I write often, but some are not comfortable with the act of sharing their thoughts, insight, and wisdom to a list of relative strangers. Sometimes people just don't know what to say.

So, what should you write about? The first thing to get clear about is that you don't need to write a lot. The number of words is less important than how you connect with your people on a level beyond, *hey, buy my stuff*.

I write long-form content for my newsletters because I dig

it. My posts almost always revolve around the subject of success for creative business owners (big surprise), but I deviate every now and then just to shake things up. I've written about the birth of my son, the emotions around getting laid off, and how my first European vacation affected me as a creative. I'll write about health and fitness, pop culture, music or anything else that rolls around in my head, but I always tie it back to the main theme of helping creatives with their work. These ideas work for me, but you have to decide for yourself what will serve your readers best.

Going back to your ICA, it's important to understand who you are writing to, and what their motivation was for signing up for your list. Were they hoping for insights on how you do the work you do, or do they want to know when you post new stuff? Do they want a backstage pass to how you operate your daily life, or do they want your opinions on the industry. Your top priority is fulfilling the promise you gave the readers when they signed up. If you told them you would send updates of new products, sending out a post that talks about your daily life might not be what they want to read about. Consider your people, then define the parameters about what topics you cover. If they know going in that it might be a mix of things, then you won't have a problem. Also, with technology today, you can group people into different categories, submitting messages only to certain groups, depending on the message. If someone only wants updates about product offerings, you can put them in that group. If they want tips on how to do what you do, that's another group. Set it up right from the start and give people the choice about the kinds of information they can get from you. This is also helpful for identifying who your true customers are, who want to learn from you and be entertained.

If you know who you want to talk to, and how often you want to post, figuring out what to share is simple. First rule: It shouldn't' be a pitch fest! Some retail brands can get away with sending out messages that only sell, but chances are, those brands are offering up some form of compensation for the readers' time, maybe a small piece about how to use their products, or a coupon that only goes out to subscribers. Those are all great ideas, and you should consider them, but also think about how you can enrich the lives of the readers. Can you give something away that's free, whether that be knowledge, or even an item? A popular technique is to give away monthly desktop wallpapers, or design templates, if that's what your reader likes. A jeweler may give away a guide on how to accessorize an outfit with their latest pieces, or maybe it's tips on how to pick the right piece for a loved one. A designer could give away design tips on video, and someone who design clothes can share a fashion guide for each season. Think about your products, and figure out what your reader would love to get, and then give it away freely.

I once saw a small business owner provide a report in her newsletter of all the major recent happenings in her industry, namely the cost of doing business. She didn't come right out and say she was raising her prices, but if I had to guess, it seemed like she was prepping customers for a price increase. I'm not sure if she planned on giving that kind of report again this year, but if she created a more in-depth annual report, it could become a resource that people in her industry find useful. Valuable information like that gets shared with others, making her an authority people trust. There are no rules about what can be shared, but to dig deeper and provide value. Value is relative to your readers, but here are a few ideas to get you started:

- Post up progress photos and final shots of new work available in your shop.
- Let subscribers know if you're attending events locally, or out of town. Perhaps give a special code for a discount at that event.
- Share updates on experiments you're playing with in your work. Post some photos, and ask people what they think.
- Ask your subscribers if they have any questions about the work you do. The next update(s) should be the answers to those questions.
- Talk about changes in the industry, either from a maker, or a consumer standpoint. Express an opinion, and people will resonate with you. Take the opportunity to ask people for their thoughts. Start a conversation.
- Write about your personal experience selling, maybe top tips about what you've found successful.
- Showcase the work of people you admire. Do a Top Ten post of your favorite makers. Go deeper and pick out separate niches to focus on, and you could have content for several updates.
- Take that idea above and do a list post on just about anything that relates to your business (tools, online resources).

- Give a shop tour by sharing all the tools and products you use to do the work you do.
- Start a tutorial series in which you show your process for a large project, or even small tips you've discovered that helped with productivity.
- Share your reading list. (Hint: this book should be on it)
- Do a one-on-one interview with a fellow business person.
- Share the story of a featured customer or subscriber.
- Send a post offering big discounts on items you're trying to closeout.
- Ask people to share pics of the things they've bought, and then give a coupon to them and a friend.
- Send out a list of recent posts from other blogs that you've read and found insightful or inspiring.
- Write about your history as a creative, and how you got started.
- Write about the history of the type of work you do.
- Hold a contest where people can win something from your shop. Encourage sharing.
- Once or twice a year, say thank you to all your fans.

The limits only go as far as your own imagination. If you're ever stuck for ideas, look to websites and blogs that you enjoy and dig through their content for inspiration. Don't outright copy, but take these templates and turn them into a post specifically for your people. As long as you stay on message, and maintain trust and consistency, you can post almost anything and people will eat it up.

A side note on people who unsubscribe from your list: This will happen, often. Do not get turned off by it. It's the nature of things, and it's rarely personal. Just because someone decided to opt out of your emails does not mean they hate you. It's more likely that they just need to declutter their inbox. The important thing to remember is that these people are not your ICA. If they bail on your list, then they probably weren't going to buy from you, even if they had in the past. All you did was clear the way for someone more appropriate to take their place, someone you'd rather be talking to anyway.

KEEP THE SHIP STRAIGHT

If an email list is the wind that pushes your business across the ocean, then your website is the boat. The boat won't move without the wind, but the wind does no good if the boat isn't seaworthy. If you haven't guessed by now, I have an affinity for transportation metaphors.

If your email list is top priority, the second most important thing you should be working on is the space where people buy your stuff. Whether that's a marketplace like Etsy or Amazon, or your own site built with an e-commerce platform; managing your product offerings should be your next priority after your email list. You can market to people until you fall over from social media overload, but if you don't have somewhere to send people to buy your work, then what is the point?

If you're reading this, I assume you have made at least some sales, and by my genius powers of deduction, you have some online platform to make that happen. If you don't have an online shop presence anywhere, put this book down right now and go find one. If you make handmade goods, get on Etsy right now. If not, Etsy, try Artfire or Cargoh or any one of the other options. For a small monthly fee, you can have a Squarespace site set up in a matter of minutes, including posting items for sale. If you don't have a shop, I'm completely serious, do not do anything else until you get one started. The rest of what we're talking about is going to require you have some place for people to buy, so you better get that started right now. Go ahead—we'll wait.

Now that we're all up to speed on selling, the question remains, how effective is your shop? If you're just getting started, this will be easier, but established sellers should do a thorough assessment of their shop and offerings. It's time to ask the tough questions about your shop that lead to a better sales experience, both for you, and the customer.

Are you taking advantage of all the tools you have at your disposal? Can you optimize your listings for better buying opportunities? Product titles, descriptions, and keywords or tags can maximize your effectiveness, but there's a science to it, and it's amorphous. When writing your titles and descriptions, or picking keywords, it's important to think like a consumer. How people find your product when they don't know they want it is a honed skill that takes a lot of practice. Also, the information we have about what works today will change as web search functionality changes.

Maybe you need an image overhaul. Can you reshoot images to make them pop better? Your product photos are the first interaction with most customers, so why would you post something that sucks? Learn to take better photos, and then experiment with new ways to shoot your products that show off the facets in a compelling way.

Is your product line up to date? Do you need to add new designs based on current trends? I don't like the idea of chasing fads, but styles and trends change, and you don't want to be left hanging onto antiquated ideas in your product line. If your work needs refreshing, test out new ideas with readers and see what hits. Collect some market research by sending out a newsletter update asking your readers what they think of the ideas first. On the other side of the trends conversation, there's something to be said for brands who stick to their guns on style. They may hit a dip as their style fades, but they could eventually be thought of as *retro*, getting a resurgence in popularity when the trend comes back around.

If you are looking at a product refresh, don't be afraid to cut dead weight. If you can cut some products from your line to give some air to your shop, be ruthless about it. It's easy for creatives to get attached to the work, but you must be honest with yourself about items that don't sell. If a design is not appealing to customers, having it on display could be enough to deter them from buying anything else. Taking dead stock out of the shop can give the remaining product line a new outlook merely by disassociation.

This is your time to be brutal with your site, trim the fat, add elements where needed, and make the whole process of buying more streamlined. Remove the emotion from your work for a bit, and think like a merchandiser. When you go to a grocery or department store, all the products are placed around the room in a strategic way because the stores understand the shopping habits of customers. Items that sell well get put up front, and those that don't get pushed to the back, or taken from the shelves. They don't get attached to the products because the goal is to sell, and if it doesn't sell, it goes away. You will have more attachment to your product line than a department store—I should hope so— but don't be so attached that you can't make the tough decisions about selling and merchandising when needed.

Once you make some changes to the shop, send a note to your subscribers asking what they think of your updates. Create a questionnaire for them to fill out and give their opinions anonymously. You'll want to include basic demographic information in the questionnaire so you can identify your ICA (age, sex, location), but make it safe for your readers to speak their mind freely. Also, be very specific about what you want to know. Ask questions like, *how easy or difficult is it to navigate the site, what was your purchasing experience,* or *is there anything on the site that distracts you*? Having this insider information is invaluable, and could make the difference between a good selling season and great one. A caveat to this approach is that you want to take the information with caution. Don't dive into every suggestion readers make, because those suggestions may be in direct conflict with others. Each person who responds is coming to the questionnaire from a different perspective and life experience, so their points of view will be personally skewed. Also, they may not have the selling experience you do, and they don't fully understand the dynamics of your business. Collect the information, find the common threads, and then discern which elements you can implement to net some return.

You may find people think your site or shop needs big upgrades to improve the functionality. Your navigation or buying process may be cumbersome, and customers have no patience for sticking around. Maybe they only visit your blog for the stories you share, but not to purchase products, for whatever reason. If a complete re-do of the site is required, then maybe Squarespace, Shopify, or MadeFreshly is in your future. This may be news you don't want to hear, but if the current shop keeps you from sales, then you need to get on that problem right away.

If you're on Etsy or Shopify, then you have some analytics embedded. That's good, and you should use them. If you're operating on a platform that doesn't have analytics installed, I suggest getting that in order soon so you can track visitors and traffic sources. You don't need to be exhaustive about this, but it's good to know where and how people are using your site. The Resource Guide in the back of the book lists a few options for you to check out.

If you feel good about your site's functionality, and you feel like the traffic is decent, but could use improvement, then it may come down to the quality of your content and promotional efforts. Which posts got the most attention? Was there a consistent theme to the posts that got readers inspired? Moreover, was there a theme to the posts that got ignored? If you added new items to the shop, which ones got the most traffic? Which items made the most sales? If certain products were hitting harder than others, maybe it's time for a price adjustment on the popular pieces, or a closeout discount on the ones that didn't sell.

Finally, remember that done is better than perfect. As with

anything in this book, we can overthink the things we want to change on our sites. I could spend weeks tweaking my site to make it better, but all that time I spend tweaking will keep me away from creating the content for my fans. If you're tweaking things, make a list about small projects to tackle, and make those happen over time. Don't dwell, and don't get caught up in the details. Fix something, test something. Fix it again, test again, and then move on. As important as it is to make your site functional and effective, it's more important that you go make cool stuff, and then find ways to sell it.

HOW SOCIAL ARE YOU, REALLY?

If you're like me, you're just about social'd out after the holidays. If I have to go to one more party filled with people I don't know, having to explain to them what I do, I might choke myself with a fruitcake. The thought of jumping back onto Facebook and Twitter after Christmas to promote gives me hives. Instead, using that tense energy to my advantage, post-holidays is the perfect time for me to cull the social herd. On every social network, I always end up following way more people than necessary. We get caught up in chasing a higher follower count, but to what end? The result is a more cluttered feed, and I'm too distracted to interact with the people I want to maintain real relationships with. Granted, I am always willing to interact with fans and followers. I love the people who reach out to me, every one of them, and I embrace their interactions. However, the things they post in their social media feeds are not always inline with my own interests. Am I obligated to follow all of them because they follow me? No, I'm not.

The reality is that a good portion of the people who track you in social media don't actually want to be your customer. Just like email lists, if you lose followers because they aren't interested in what you're sharing, then they weren't your true fans anyway. You might as well move on and find people that relate to you, and will become your best customer evangelists.

Since you're already sucked into a social media vortex, why not take some time to reduce the number of folks who borrow your attention, especially if you don't want what they are sharing? You'll be doing them a favor because you're likely not their ICA, so why clutter up their true list of fans? It's not personal, just a cleaning up of clutter. If you look at this pragmatically, it can be good for everyone in the end.

On the other side of the social media conversation, take time to review your efforts on the various platforms. It's common to have a presence in every platform, and I believe you should, but perhaps now is a good time to consider where you should be spending most of your time online. Some people say Twitter is huge for their business, but I've never had much luck there aside from the interactions of a few true friends. Facebook is falling out of favor with many small businesses. To compete, it's a pay-for-play situation. You need to buy Facebook ads in order to get attention from others, and many people feel they can't get the reach they need with spending a ton of money on promotion. Facebook works for me to a degree, and I feel like I get good interaction in my groups, but is it the best use of my time?

With most creative businesses, visual identity is important, and that means looking at visual sites like Pinterest, Instagram, and Tumblr. I have a presence on each one, but truthfully only spend time on Instagram with any regularity. I loved Pinterest at the beginning, but find it too distracting to spend time there on a consistent basis. Some of my colleagues say that Pinterest is essential to their business, and they don't mind getting sucked in if it means they get to sell more through it. If it works for you, then you should work it for all its worth. You have one or two outlets that work best for your business. Take the opportunity to look at your social options more closely and decide where your time is best spent. If Facebook doesn't work for your business, why would you spend time there? I like Twitter, but I won't be killing myself to use it. Instead, I develop a plan that allows me to interact in small bits, and not worry about all my different accounts after fifteen minutes of engagement. Be vigilant in your efforts, and if you have time to spend on the others, by all means, go share, as long as you don't spend all day there.

FURTHER DOWN THE SPIRAL

Here in Southern California, we have a supermarket chain called Food 4 Less. It's not my favorite place to shop because they don't have much of a selection when it comes to healthy choices, but they serve a particular section of the local demographic, and they do it well.

Unlike most supermarkets, where you enter and can roam free in any direction you choose; when you first walk into a Food4Less, they lead you down a corridor of popular products and brands. They know what people buy most, and they make sure those are the items you see first. While they've got you in the sales corridor, they share other brands that you may not know about, but sell at a better price margin for the store. The deals are irresistible, and Food4Less knows you'll buy something in that corridor if they can entice you to put it in your cart. This corridor snakes around and dumps you out at the back of the store, where you can then carry on with any of your regular shopping. You just have to make your way down at least one more aisle before you can check out. You may not have noticed but you walked your way through the physical representation of a sales funnel. Some might see that process as manipulative, but others might see it as efficient selling people who were in shopping mode already. I do not endorse the many of the products sold by Food4Less, but the science of how they put things in front of you is something to consider in your own business.

Nobody knows shopping habits quite like supermarket chains. They know you are going to visit about once a week, and they are watching your every move while you shop to figure out your habits. The perishable items like meat, eggs, and milk are always at the back of the store because they are things people come in to buy most often. Putting those items at the back of the store forces you to walk down the aisles of other products, maybe gathering up items in an impulse purchase.

At the front of the store, the end caps and point-of-sale items you see at any market or department store are there because retailers know there might be one last, little thing to tempt you, whether it's a candy bar, a magazine, or a pair of nail clippers. You may not buy anything there, but while you're waiting to check out, you're being tempted by that Snickers bar or *People* magazine, and it was all done by design.

You would think that the Food4Less sales stopped there, but oh no. Soon, in your mailbox, you'll get a flyer from them, telling you about all the special deals they have for shoppers in your area. If you sign up for a loyalty program, you get special coupons in the mail directed right at your shopping habits. You'll also get a weekly email from them, presenting loss-leader deals that get you into the store to go through the process all over again. You could opt-out of all those, but chances are you won't, and they know it. It's anthropological at the core, and since you're human, there's not much you can do but absorb the science and learn from it.

Ask yourself, how do you use this to your benefit? How can

you get people through your own sales funnel while maintaining the integrity of the brand you've worked hard to build up? There is no one right answer for everyone, but let's run down some scenarios, and perhaps you can apply the ideas to your own business in a seamless way that benefits both you and your customers. You don't want to be slimy or insidious in your approach, but you should want to capitalize on the human nature of consumers. Do customers *need* to buy more of your stuff? Probably not, but it would definitely feel good to have them pick up one more item, making your overall profit a bit higher.

Any sales funnel is made up of three parts: how to get them to your shop, how to drive them through the shop to buy more stuff, and how to follow up for future sales, Try to keep in mind the ideas I discussed earlier about your brand experience, and how that will come into play as a potential customer makes their way through your world.

A Trip to the Store

Every customer's journey begins at a gate, an entry point into your space. It might be your shop, blog, social media, or maybe in person. If it is your booth or shop—well done! We'll talk about those folks in a moment, but for the lookie-loos, scanning your social outlets, we need to entice them forward. Ask yourself, what is the thing they want to see from you most, and how do you give it to them? The more you put up nice pictures on your blog and in social media, the more likely they are to get shared. Enough pretty pictures in a row, or compelling conversations, and people will want to dig further.

Your social media outlets mention your blog, your blog mentions your newsletter, and your newsletter takes people to your shop. Sure, you can send people direct from Twitter or Facebook to your shop, but there's no enticement. The goal is to drive them from passive attention span (social) into more active attention span (email). People who make it that far will want more of your awesomeness, so they sign up for it to find out about your work, your process, your adventures, and your insights. For those doubters who ask themselves, *why would they want to hear from me?* take heed. People do want to know what you think about things. You may not think they want to hear what you have to say, but I guarantee, they do.

Your newsletter goes out once a week into their inbox, but on average, only about forty percent open it (which makes it even more important to stay on schedule), so you focus your energy on talking to them about subjects you know they want to hear most. While you have them there, you can mention some new items you have in the shop, a sales you have coming, or events you're attending, or give them a coupon that expires in a short period. Maybe you're collaborating with another shop owner that complements your products, and together you post about the newly formed—and perhaps limited edition—collaboration. The customers jump on that train and head over to your shop to snatch it up.

The train metaphor works because it's your job to move them from one spot, to the next. Not only are you immersing them in all that you do, but you're creating trust and loyalty with each interaction. Sometimes they want a high-speed train ride direct to their destination, but most want to take their time getting there. Be a good steward and give them reasons to stay on the train.

Browsing the Racks at High Speed

In a physical store, it's easy to put things in front of shoppers so they might buy something on impulse. On the Internet, that's not always so easy. You may have a limited window to gain their attention. Even if you do have their attention, the time you have is short. Imagine a ticking stopwatch every time someone enters your store. You have less than thirty seconds to wow them enough to browse further. If they do stick around, you have on average of ninety more seconds to keep them engaged. There's not a lot you can do in that time, so your efforts need to be concise and to the point. The best advice is still pretty pictures with searchable titles, relatable descriptions, and a smooth transition between pages and sections—do not make your visitors think, and do not make them work.

Your navigation should be perfectly clear. If you have your own shop with a blog and other pages, make sure you shop link is easily identified. If you are on a marketplace like Etsy, your categories should read as if someone was searching for those terms exactly. Do not be cheeky or glib with your categories or navigation because people will bounce if they don't understand it right off. Think about how department stores are set up. Could you ever imagine going into Macy's and seeing all the items in the store categorized by color or price point first? People do not go into a department store asking, "Where is the *Under $50* section? Macy's would never entertain that idea, so why would you?

Compartmentalization is good, and the more you can compartmentalize items, the better. However, don't break it down so much that people have to sift through tons of categories to find what they want. You want to make finding things easy, and not overwhelming. Once they click into a category, put your best sellers at the top intermixed with items that contrast or complement. If you have combos featuring your best sellers and others, those work great too. When someone clicks through to an item, start thinking how you can get them to the next item before they bounce. Maybe there's something in your listing that says, *you might also like...*, or link that states, *see this item in another color*. Perhaps in one of your picture options, you post something that shows a similar item and leads them there, shows the items in a different colors, or gives them some call to action. The idea is to keep them moving through the listing until they hit the Buy button. The longer you can keep them in your shop, the better.

Another high-level approach is to give them options for secondary purchases after they have added something to their shopping cart. Not all marketplaces do this effectively, if at all, so it may not be an option, but if there is something you can do to add that functionality, use it. If it works for Amazon, why wouldn't it work for you?

I also recommend prompting people to share your items on social media. If you can add a Pinterest, Twitter, or Facebook like button on an item, do so. If you can get people to share their purchases through those outlets, by all means, hit them up. If someone is truly happy with their purchasing experience, they will share it. The longer people stay in your shop, the more likely they will buy and share, and then you get a chance to put a new person on the train.

After the Drop

Ok, you made some sales in January. Woot, woot! I hope they were big ones. Now are you just going to let those people slip through your fingers, hoping they return someday? Most shops will do the cliché thing of sending a postcard along with their item that gives a thank you and perhaps a discount code for the future. That's a nice gesture, and I recommend it, but if that's all you're doing, then you're not doing enough.

There is some discrepancy about whether you should have the right to add a buyer to your email list. The truth is that you can't legally add someone to your list unless they gave you some sort of permission to be there. Now, if what you're selling is based on email interaction, like what I do, then you're in the clear, but if you're selling products, people need to know they are being added to the list. One suggestion is to follow up with someone one time via email to thank them for their purchase, and then share a link to your newsletter signup. If you're using a bigger e-commerce platform, you might have the capability to include an opt-in box on the shopping cart or receipt page.

Also, just because you may have their permission does not mean you should email them anything you want. If you have a newsletter, where people come for the core content about building a business, sending them to that list is not a disconnect. However, if they bought one of your products, and then you send them to a lifestyle and how-to type of newsletter, they may call you out as a spammer. If you do get permission to add a customer to your list, perhaps segmenting your list in a way that you can talk directly to them as former customers, and send them only the content that reflects their purchase, and future purchases. If there is a way to segment a customer further, based on what they purchased, you could serve them messages about specific products that might be of interest to them. If you make leather handbags, you probably don't want to shove messages into their inbox trying to get them to buy more leather handbags, but if you can share with them some new accessories to go with it, that might be useful, or maybe encourage them to buy a bag for a friend. Maybe you partner with a scarf maker, or a jewelry designer, and you send out a bulk message to your people with that collaboration. These are endemic messages, and are well within the realm of proper email etiquette.

Take great care in how your message is crafted, making sure you don't say something that feels contrived. If a message feels inauthentic to you, that's going to come across in the message. Don't follow the trends of others—do what feels real to you. If it's not something you would personally respond to as a buyer, then don't use it in your message. Each interaction with you is a plus or minus in the branding column, so do your best to add pluses and minimize minuses.

Also, make sure your Unsubscribe button or link is prominent on the page so people can opt out easily. You do not want them adding you to their spam folder because they couldn't find the button to stop receiving messages from you. Getting marked as spam is inevitable because some people will be too click-happy, or too lazy to find the proper unsubscribe link. Anyone who has a newsletter has been marked by someone as spam at one point. The email service providers know this, but if you're getting marked as spam each time you send out a note, then you're going to get dinged hard, and maybe lose your service altogether.

Sales Funnel in Action

I use the term *product* throughout this bit because I want you to associate the thinking to whatever it is you sell. My product for this example is this book. While you're reading, I want you to keep an open mind as to how what I'm saying can still apply to your items. Some aspects may not apply directly, but if you think about them deeper, the answer will present itself.

Breaking down how I get products or offerings into the hands of new people, it all starts with social media tease. I test the concept with people by giving hints to my idea, or asking questions that revolve around what I think people want to know more about. Those questions not only help me gauge interest, but they give me tips on what type of content I need to focus on. Some of what you're reading is based on concerns people have shared with me.

I write blog posts that revolve around some of the book's content, and I'll post those up over time. Those posts may go into newsletters instead, because I like to spread the love around, and my newsletter people should get exclusive content more often than others.

I create graphics to share on social media, even if they don't lead to a product yet. The idea is to create a product profile for people to understand where I'm headed, even if it's not clear from the start. Each tease eludes to something bigger, and not only does this boost anticipation, but it builds up my professional perception in that area. This is beneficial for me, because even if I may be an expert in a particular area, if I hadn't talked about it before this point, there will be a disconnect with people. While writing this book, someone quizzed me that they didn't see me as an expert in selling products, and thought there was a disconnect between the book and my skill. It was a valid concern, and I thanked her for the insight, but then I reassured her of my past experience, and also shared that although the book is about selling, the core of what the content is about relates to branding. It made sense to her after that, but I realized that there was a problem with how I was sharing the content. Even us would-be experts need a proverbial gut check once in a while to remind us we don't have it all figured out, and I will continue to work on fixing the disconnect.

Once my product is built and close to launch, I share the visuals with people, letting them know the name and subject of the project. I share the links on my blog, newsletter, podcast, and social media over and over and over again. I try not to be spammy, using incremental posting discretion depending on the outlet, but I know that not everyone sees my messages when I first put them out, so I share and share again.

Once the product is available, I share the full version with everyone, and give them options for buying. Not all people want to consume content in the same way, and providing options, both in actual product, and where it's sold, I expand my reach and potential sales. I also offer add-ons that people can buy from my site directly, and the information for getting those add-ons is in the book itself.

Now that you're holding onto the content, and you've read through it, there are references to my other materials and projects in the back. These are linked in the Appendix, and you might be enticed to pick them up as well. Of course, when you buy and read those items, there are links back to this one, because that's essential to the sales loop.

Many of you may have seen the opt-in at the front and the back of the book, and are now on my list (as you should be, because why wouldn't you want to be). I send you content revolving around what I talk about here, peppered with new potential offerings. I share my other media outlets, and I ask people to share what they've read, seen, or heard with others they know who might benefit. If those new people come over, then I start the cycle all over again. It's a continuous operation, so anytime someone gets into the loop, they are always going to get introductory-level content and work their way up to any of my more advanced content.

Because this product is digital (even if you're holding the print copy), I can make changes on the fly and upgrade the content. This may be my flagship content when I first launch, but soon it won't be, and I will do what I can to keep people's interest in the newer, bigger, better thing.

With every stage of what I am doing, I am always asking myself how I can move people organically down the line in order to benefit them. Over time, I will produce different niche

Best Practices : 100

content that will hit certain people more acutely than others, Not everyone on my list will be interested, but I know I can make that transition because I'm always asking question and always posting ideas. The ones that get the most traction are the ones that get my attention, and then become the ones you see more of in the future.

Don't worry, I'm not pitching you on anything else... yet.

THE PRICE IS ALMOST RIGHT

Let's talk about pricing for a brief moment, and this will probably the briefest section in this chapter, because the subject is both simple and difficult, which causes me to avoid an exhaustive dialog.

The simple fact is that you are not charging enough for your work. I can say this with confidence because I have talked with hundreds of creative business owners and ninety-five percent of the time, they are not charging enough for their work. It's a plague, and it's brought on by a combination of competition, comparison, and limiting self-belief.

Many people charge too little for their work because they are trying to keep in line with their competition. They see their competition on Etsy, or at festivals, and they base their pricing on what they see, never considering for a moment that the people they are comparing themselves to are doing the same thing. Everyone is copying what others are doing, but few have taken the time to consider the possibility that customers could and would pay more.

Others don't charge enough because they do not believe in the value of their work. They might start by looking at what their competition charges, but then mark their prices down because they don't believe they are on the same level. They question their own worth, and assume customers will not pay the true value of the work.

Recently, I went to a handmade festival, and I ran across a woman who made ornate, felted scarves. The detail that went into each piece was incredible, and probably took her several hours to create, but she was only charging forty-five dollars for them. I would never tell someone who didn't ask that they weren't charging enough, but I wanted to at that moment. Instead, I walked away thinking she doesn't take her work seriously. Some might say she is charging what the market would bear, but my thought is that the market needs to bear a little more, and pay her what she's worth. That doesn't mean she must double or triple her prices overnight, but it wouldn't be a bad idea.

Instead of getting down on anyone about pricing—and without judging your pricing mindset, I would ask you to make a commitment to yourself right now. If you haven't changed your prices in a while, go into your shop and raise your prices ten percent. Don't hesitate, don't balk, and don't ask questions. Just go in and change it right now. You know what's going to happen? Nothing! People will still buy from you, and you will still sell the same, but now you're making ten percent more.

I believe every creative business owner should be raising their prices at least five to ten percent a year on average. The cost of doing business goes up year to year, so why shouldn't your prices? Some could raise them more than that and be fine, but 10-percent won't hurt anyone, and you'll be ten percent richer this time next year.

PLAY TO YOUR STRENGTHS— DELEGATE YOUR WEAKNESSES

Let's face it, there are some things in your business you're just not good at. Maybe you're not good at graphic design, writing copy, tracking expenses, or managing inventory. Instead of outsourcing these projects, the half-effort you make on them is doing your business a disservice.

You might be crippling your business out of an antiquated ideology that you must run your shop by yourself in order to remain pure and authentic to your craft. It's not an uncommon thought, but one based in scarcity. You might believe you can't afford to outsource, but allow me to illustrate that you can't not afford to outsource the heavy lifting in areas where you are weakest.

Imagine for a moment, that you pay yourself a rate of $50 an hour. That's $50 an hour for all the creative work, the bookkeeping, the social media updates, stocking the shelves, and taking out the garbage. Can you imagine paying someone to come to your studio to tidy up for $50 an hour? Of course not, but you do every day because you're acting as the tidy-upper, and we already established the amount you're paying yourself.

Now imagine you hired someone to come in and do your social media, stock your shelves, and fulfill orders for $25 an hour. Not only are you paying less overall, but they might be able to do it faster than you, since they aren't splitting their time between other things. Now you can focus your fifty dollars an hour energy on projects that warrant that cost, like new concepts and creativity.

Maybe you're not making enough money to pay anyone yet, but consider for a moment that there are small things in your business you might be able to delegate or pay a freelancer to do for you. For instance, I am considering adding text transcripts of all my podcast episodes. Am I going to type out each episode myself? I could, but why do that when I can pay someone to do it cheaper and faster than I could?

Another friend of mine runs a greeting card business. She takes great pride in the quality of the paper and envelopes she uses for her greeting cards, but because of that, she had to print, fold, and package every card herself. In the past, I tried to convince her that as she grew, she would be able to save time and money by outsourcing her printing. Her thought was if she didn't have her hands on the product, then it was no longer handmade, and therefore not valid. As her business grew, so did her workload, and at some point in the past year, she finally decided to outsource the printing of her cards. She still assembles and packages the items herself, but by sending the printing out, she saves time that is best spent creating new designs.

So, from now on, anytime you consider working on a new project in your business, take a moment to ask yourself, *is this a $50 an hour job or not*, and if the answer is no, then it's time to add that task that to the list of things you should be outsourcing.

OPEN MIND / NARROW FOCUS

One of the mistakes some small brands make is trying to make a push too early into bigger territory by expanding their lines. The common thought is that if they are having some reasonable success with five products, then ten products will make them even more money, but this is rarely the case. Sure, they may make a little more money than they did before, but because of all the extra time and energy spent to develop, make, and promote new product lines, it's rarely profitable until a considerable amount of time down the road. Unfortunately, before they can wait for that time to come, they're looking to expand again. Exponential growth by adding more product lines seems like a good idea when you're in it, but at some point you will reach a critical mass that keeps you from getting ahead of your business because you're trying to manage too many products at once.

Instead of expanding into new lines, I often recommend business owners do the opposite and narrow their focus, maintain or reduce their product offerings so they can portray themselves as a specialist in a given area. There are plenty jack-of-all-trades in the creative world, all competing for space, but imagine if you specialized in a given area that allowed you the chance to set yourself apart from the crowd. Narrowing your focus to become the champion of the one thing that you do best could give you the leg up you are looking for in this battle for attention.

Back in the 1950s, Southern California fast food was dominated by two congenial yet opposing forces. On one side was Carls Jr., and on the other side was McDonalds. Both founders, Carl Karcher and Ray Kroc, respectively, had mutual respect for each other, but they were also fierce competitors, going at each other's businesses to see who could dominate the Southland. While those two were going at it, a quiet man by the name of Harry Snyder had a plan to open his own small burger chain. His plan was to keep things really simple: burgers, fries, and shakes. Instead of adding to the menu for more growth whenever he saw a need, he instead focused on creating the best possible product he could. He grew his company slow and steady, as opposed to McDonald's and Carl's, which grew at exponential rates. Snyder focused more on the infrastructure of his company, buying high-quality meat, baking his own buns, and using food that was never frozen. He made quality food at a reasonable price, and made sure his customers were happy.

More than fifty years later and In-n-Out burger maintains one of the best reputations in the entire world for fast, yet high-quality food. Over the past decade, they have started to move beyond the California border, and whenever they enter a new locale, the crowds reach legendary proportions, maintaining that level for months on end. In California, In-n-Out is as ubiquitous as the ocean breeze, commonplace to some regard, yet it's a rare occasion that I set foot into one and it's not busy. In-n-Out built one of the most notable food brands in the world, and they did so with a simple ideology: Make high-quality, simple food, and provide great service. That's a formula that just about anybody could implement in their business and be successful, and you don't even have to cut up any onions.

Conversely, another California company took a similar approach to making shoes. In 1966, the Van Doren brothers and their partners opened the Van Doren Rubber company, where they sold their handmade shoes direct to the public. They didn't have a lot of designs, or fancy colors. In fact, they had exactly one shoe style back then with limited colors, and that same shoe is still one of the most popular styles today. Once the surfers and skaters took hold of the shoe as the standard footwear of the beach culture, the Van Doren brothers never looked back, and "Man, I need Vans," became a rally cry of anyone who wanted to be part of the California sunshine.

Vans Shoes is one of the largest shoe manufacturers in the country, and has since diversified its line a lot, but they started small, stayed simple, and always stuck to their roots. They're not out trying to create the next cross trainer or running shoe. They don't make loafers or boots, unless it's snow boots for traversing mountaintops to board down. The aesthetic that Vans created is so robust and popular that the big dogs in the category, Nike, Puma and Converse all have tried to move in on the action sports industry. While those companies fight over the scraps, Vans keeps doing what they've always done; making cool shoes that embody a lifestyle that everybody wants.

Husqvarna Motorcycles is another example of a company that had an opportunity to become a massive supplier of two-wheeled transportation, but when the motocross industry started to grow in the early 1970s, *Huskie*, as the company is referred to by loyalists, chooses to stick to what they knew, which is off-road vehicles. While other companies like Honda, Kawasaki, and Yamaha were expanding their lines in every direction, Husqvarna stayed true to making the most reliable motocross bikes around. Today they have a total of fifteen different motorcycles that vary only in size for different riders and riding styles. They don't have a street bike line, or a touring motorcycle line. They don't make street fighters, cafe racers, cruisers or trials bikes. The do what they do, and they do it well.

Huskies aren't cheap, and the maintenance costs are legendary, but the people who buy them know what they are buying. Husqvarna recognizes their place in the market and they have no intention of relinquishing their title as the ultimate off-road motorcycles.

You may not care about hamburgers, casual footwear, or off road motorcycles, but I'm sure you can relate to the idea these companies embody. Fewer products, more specialization, and a focus on quality craftsmanship are what sets these companies apart from their competitors. When the rest of the world suffers from the ebb and flow of market fluctuation, these companies thrive because they know their market, and they cater to it in the best way they see fit. You don't have to be a biker, a surfer, or a Californian to recognize that.

DO PEOPLE WANT WHAT YOU'RE SELLING?

The other day I had an enlightening conversation with my friend Rena Tom, of Makeshift Society, about small-business retail sellers. The most profound thought coming out of that conversation was that many artists, designers, and makers do not know what makes a person buy what they are selling. They make products based on whims and inspiration, which is great for artistic vision, but may not be a viable business model. Selling isn't that difficult if you know the secrets, but it seems to be an elusive beast for many creative folks.

Do you want to know the big secret to selling, the one that can change your entire perspective on how people see your work? It's a really simple concept that many of you may have heard but don't take into account when launching new items.

People Do Not Buy Things...

They may want your stuff, may love your stuff, but they didn't buy it because it was nice, pretty, well made, or a good value. They bought that thing because they knew it was going to make them feel good about themselves, or serve a specific purpose that improves their life in some way.

Everyone knows the cliché that women love buying shoes. Not many would disagree, but do women really love the act of buying the shoes? Does picking up a box of shoes, taking it to the counter, running their credit card, and walking out of the store with the box in a bag make them excited, anxious, or nervous? Does the buying process make them feel confident and sexy? Not hardly, but the shoes definitely do those things.

Women don't buy sexy, strappy, 5-inch heels because they're cute. The shoes may be cute, but those shoes may not be that cute to wear for more than an hour or so.

They bought the shoes because of how the shoes made them look and feel when they looked at them in the mirror. Their feet looked small, they're legs looked long, and their butt made them think Jennifer Lopez walked in the room. They bought those shoes because for every moment they are in them, a small ember burns sexy confidence inside, and they want to feel that slow burn as often as they can.

...They Buy How Your Things Make Them Feel.

Recently I bought a poster for my son from a local artist. It was a nice illustration with dinosaurs on it, and it matches the color palette of my son's room. Did I buy the poster because he loves dinosaurs? Did I buy it because it matches his room? Did I buy it because I believe it's important to support the community of independent artists and creators that I serve? My son does love dinosaurs, the poster does match the room, and I do want to support an independent artist, but that's not what got me to pull out my wallet. I bought the poster for self-serving reasons, all of which were calculated in my head without me thinking about them for more than a millisecond.

First, I knew if I brought home a poster, my wife would be happy that I did something for my son. My boy would be happy and think I was the best dad in the world. The woman I bought the poster from would be happy she made another sale and I get to put a feather in my cap about making her day a little better. The question for the artist is, how can she capitalize on those facts? What can she do with her business that helps me get to that buying decision easier?

It's important for you to take some time and think about how your products make people feel about themselves when they buy. If you don't know, you should ask people. Ask friends, family members, or even past customers what it is about products like yours that make them buy. Don't let them get away by saying how nice the items are, or how it's a good value. Why is value important? What does a pretty object make them feel inside? What thoughts are created in their minds when buying something for themselves or others? A process I like to implement is called the *Three Whys*, where you ask a question of someone, and then you get them to dig deeper by asking them why two or three more times.

"Why did you buy that piece of art?"

"Because I like the picture."

"Why do like the picture?"

"Because it reminds me of home."

"Why does it remind you of home?"

"Because the house on the hill looks like my grandparent's house where I would spend my weekends and summers growing up as a kid. I love that time in my life."

No demographic information in the world is going to give you that kind of insight, and the only way to get it is by asking people to go deeper. When you tap into these gold nuggets of wisdom, then you can sell to people better. Craft your message to the feelings you want to create in your perspective buyers, connect with them on a deeper level, and they will not only buy, they will rave. Customers will share your items with their friends because they want their friends to feel the same way you made them feel.

Don't sell to them; sell into them. Make the customers need you more than they ever thought they wanted you. It takes work, and you will wrack your head over this for a while, but if you can tap into those ways, you will set yourself up for major selling success.

7

MINDSET MATTERS

Not everything we do within our business relates to the tangible aspects like marketing, production, and online creative elements. Sometimes the things we do to grow our business stem from within ourselves, and other times, come from elements beyond our walls.

Often, when we are going through the process of our daily business rituals, we run up against our own free will. We stop project midstream to chase some other less important tasks, or we hole ourselves up in our studios, avoiding the world around us, asserting that we can do this work alone. Our life is filled with obstacles; some we put up ourselves, and others pop up all on their own. How we manage these obstacles is what separates successful businesses and those that plateau and flounder.

I questioned whether I should put this chapter in the book because the subject matter extends far beyond the scope of branding, but I've found these ideas to be imperative to success. There are many tools we can use to build a thriving business, but what about the tools we have within ourselves? The problem is that we have the obstacles within ourselves, but we also have the ability to tackle the obstacles, if we put our minds to the task. Opening our minds to new ideas, and recognizing how old idea hold us back, is how we pave a path to success. What happens from there is what defines us as professionals.

FINDING SUCCESS WITH OTHERS

Some entrepreneurs have a tendency to think that it is their lot in life to go this journey alone, and when I started, I felt the same. Then one day I did something radical—I went outside. I went to an event where a bunch of makers were selling their goods, and I socialized with them. I talked with them about their work, their business, and their outlook on where the creative industry was headed. It was an insightful day on many levels.

The funny thing about that day is that it started me off on my current journey of helping other creatives. At the time, I was a frustrated artist working as an art director by day. Because my day job involved a lot of production work, I didn't have much time to express my creative energy, I thought it would go away if I didn't use the skill. I started creating art pieces of various kinds, and then went out to sell them. At the same time, I started sharing my story as a maker on my site, *Fresh Rag*, while featuring the work of other artists and designers. I soon realized the topics that people wanted to hear more about were the ones where I shared my insight on branding, marketing, and business. In November of 2012, I shifted focus, and I ventured forth to become a beacon for other creatives. That wouldn't have happened, at least not on that timeline, if I hadn't taken the time to go out and meet some of the other people doing the same kind of work.

Now I make it a point to go out on a regular basis and meet other entrepreneurs of all sorts. At least once a month, I gather a group of people together to hang out and talk business stories over food and cocktails. Without a doubt, spending time with others in business is a big part of why I move at the pace I do. I would not be as far along without those people.

The positive influences that come into your life should be added to your list of benefits, because that's exactly what they are. Friends, family members, and colleagues that support you and your venture are mandatory for positive vibes and good business health. The key word there is supportive, and it should be the determinate of who you spend your time hanging around.

SURROUND YOURSELF WITH SUCCESS

Author, Jim Rohn said, "You are the average of the five people you spend the most time with." When you hang out with smart, sophisticated, and successful entrepreneurs, guess what happens to you. Hang out in the universe, and you become a star, but if you hang out with trash, you get dirty.

I love all my friends and (most of my) family, but there are many I don't hang out with often because they do not hold the same entrepreneurial values I do. They don't share the same drive for something better than the life they live. They're stuck in their ways of working dead-end jobs, having dead-end thoughts about dead-end things, and I don't want that to be part of my daily life.

I also know artists, designers, and crafters who dwell in a mindset of scarcity. They believe they can only do business one way, and no matter how much you try to help them grow, they will not do the work. As much as I love hanging out with creative people, these folks don't bring to the table the mindset I'm trying to manifest in myself, and I choose to not hang out with them. It may sound cold and calculating, but wisely choosing the people I hang around is the reason I am able to make big things happen on a regular basis. They believe in me, so I believe in me.

Who believes in you? Think about the people you hang out with most. Do they want what you want? Do they encourage your efforts, or do they diminish your thoughts and hold you back? Do they hate on your ideas because they don't like that you're growing, changing, while they are stuck in their ways? If these *friends* sound familiar, maybe it's time for new friends.

Some people really suck! There, I said it, but it's true. These people will do everything in their power to hold you back, knock you down, and make you feel like trash for wanting more from life than their personal, predetermined *fair share*. Most will come at you anonymously, because it's easy. Other times, these people will be close friends or family members. I guarantee, the moment you read that last sentence, you already had at least one or two names pop in your head, didn't you? I can't tell you how many backhanded compliments I received the first week I announced I was not going back into the work force, but venturing out on my own instead. These people think they are doing you a service by dishing out their perspective, but the truth is they are likely jealous that you get to chase your dream, and they are too scared to consider the possibility for themselves.

You friends and family don't intentionally mean you harm—they merely don't want to see you change. They like you exactly as you are, and that's comfortable. The minute you change, you make them face the reality that "normal" is boring. They're OK with boring because it's safe. Their scarcity mindset has a firm grip on their psyche, and the only thing they know is how to be safe.

Do not let these people hold you back. They do not realize true safety comes in the form of freeing yourself from the shackles of the perceived status quo. When they come at you with their comments, just smile, thank them for their input, and let it fall off you. You have no room in your life for that baggage.

Sometimes they won't relent. They will come at you, knock you, or shun you. If that is the case, then perhaps the answer is to let them go. They should not be one of your top five, and maybe it's time to push them off the list completely. Instead find people that encourage and embolden you. That's where the magic happens.

FIND A MENTOR

One of the best things I ever did for my career was find a mentor to learn from when I was fresh out of school. In fact, I was lucky enough to have a succession of individuals who helped craft me into the professional I am today. Now I am the one that people come to for guidance, and I get the chance to give back what was given to me. I believe everyone should have the same experience. Whether it's a good friend you can emulate, a mastermind group you can join, or a training course with a proven expert in your field, make sure you get a mentor soon.

When it comes to working one-on-one with a mentor, it's not as simple as hitting someone up and asking them the occasional questions on how to run your business. There needs to be a commitment and accountability in that relationship for it to be mutually beneficial. You also need to first ask that person if they would be willing to mentor you, otherwise you're just another person asking for free advice. They may say no, so you'll find another. They may say yes, but charge a fee for the opportunity. If you can afford to pay, you should. It's an investment in your future, and you'll save that amount and then some by getting veteran experience and wisdom at your fingertips.

In 2014, I started my first mastermind group called the Fresh Rag Masters. When I started it, I knew it would be helpful to the members, but I had no idea how transformative it would become. Like the Masters group, masterminds usually have an entrance fee, meet on a regular basis, and have massive amounts of accountability. Do not join a mastermind unless you're serious about getting some insane amounts of work done. The result will be a boatload of knowledge both from peers and experts. If you're in a good group, your business life will be accelerated. You will get more done, faster, and become highly productive. The accountability of the group has to be there, and you are as responsible to hold others accountable as they will be for you. It's work, it's tough, and can be emotionally draining, but the changes will be amazing. Masterminds aren't for everyone, but if you're looking to grow your business with a family of people, this is your best option.

Some people prefer self-guided training instead. When I was part way into my business, I joined a few training programs, but the most successful of those also included a community where we could all come together to talk about the training, our successes, breakthroughs, and things we struggle with in our business. Training courses are the easiest barrier to entry, but you still must put the work in to get value out of them. You also need to give the training time to take affect long after the course is done. Results don't happen rapidly—it's a process. Some people bounce from one training to the next, constantly learning, but never applying the training. The only thing they achieve is an emptier wallet.

Whatever route you choose, make sure you're mentally, emotionally, and physically invested in the program, otherwise you're wasting your time and money. Hopefully you're serious about your business and it's worth the time and money to help it grow. I've done all of the above and I can tell you that they work if you're invested.

HANG OUT WITH PEOPLE YOU LIKE

Originally, the title of this portion was *hang out with people you don't know*, but I rewrote it knowing some introverts might have a hard time hanging out with people they don't know. I don't want to send anyone into a nervous fit at the thought of strangers, but at some point, you should try to get outside your comfort zone and meet new people. For the moment, let's stick to people we know and love. It wasn't that long ago that I found myself on the road to *shut-in* status. I wouldn't go so far to say I was a recluse, but I did have more resistance to hanging out with others. I am not exactly sure why this happened in my late thirties, but when I took a good look at my life and how unfulfilled I was, I decided to make a change.

I don't go out all the time, and when I do, it's usually one-on-one or in small groups, but even those get-togethers make a big difference in how I look at being social. These days, I will almost always take the opportunity to go hang out when people ask, even if I don't know the group that well.

Every thought leader out there will tell you that networking is one of the best things you can do for your business. Hanging out with like-minded individuals always provides some sort of gain, even if it's just an opportunity to have a good time and make new friends. Creative individuals have a tendency to hide in their space so they can focus on their work, dwell in their comfort zone, but that can be a dangerous place to hang out. If you don't pull yourself out of your hovel once in a while, you may get stuck. Next thing you know, you're Howard Hughes, growing your fingernails and wearing boxes of tissue for shoes.

Of course, there is more to it than just hanging out with creative friends. That is fun, but at some point the meet-ups should also have a strategy to them. Perhaps it's making connections that will benefit your work, or it's going to events that help you improve your business. Mentors, mastermind groups, and meet-ups can be both fun and advantages to your work, but just like spending too much time on social media, it's important to measure the purpose behind your hangout time. If you're doing it often just to be with friends, at some point, that will have a negative effect on your productivity. Go hang out, have fun, get inspired, and learn new things, but remember to take that inspiration and knowledge back to the studio for some quality creative time.

F**K FEAR!

I saved this one for last because it's a bit of a kick in the the pants, but it's for your own good. The honest truth is that every single individual reading this book, even the one who wrote it, experiences fear on a regular basis. However, the fears we have about life are usually baseless and should be ignored whenever possible.

Unless you're a police officer, soldier, X-Games participant, or a wartime news reporter, the fears we have about our daily lives are not things we need to be concerned with, because humans are strong and resilient creatures. We bounce back from the most traumatic experiences, and rarely do they kill us.

Fear is a figment of our imagination, a combination of chemicals and synapses in our brain telling us that we should be cautious when stepping forward into whatever unfamiliar situation may lie ahead. I'm no anthropologist, or scientist, but the way I've heard it told to me is when our ancestors were nomadic hunter/gatherers, there was a constant need to be on alert because *Homo Erectus* was fairly low on the food chain. Our limbic brain developed an early warning system that gave us that tingling feeling when danger was near. It kept us alert, aware, and safe from harm, because you never knew when a saber-toothed cat was around the next outcropping of rocks.

Today, we don't have the need for that kind of situational awareness unless you're dodging traffic in New York City, but even then, not so much. Our potential for harm if far less than it used to be. If you're walking through dark parking lots or alleys at night, it could be sketchy, but the majority of our lives are lived in relative safety. Our limbic brain still exists, though, and it's still trying to keep us from harm. Because our level of safety has changed, though, the limbic system has adapted, and now just tries to keep us from getting hurt in our current situations. Instead of dodging mammoths and volcanoes, you're fighting off creeps in a bar, or grasping for personal space on public transportation. It's all relative, but is it worth the level of fear we feel?

Fear Is False

That twinge of resistance you are feeling that keeps you from venturing into your next project, hanging out with a group of people you don't know well, or finishing your next book is not real. There is no reason to be fearful of these things, because even in the worst case scenario, none of them will hurt you. Sure, you could spend a lot of money on a project, or hate the new people you met, or your book doesn't sell, but you are still alive. Stepping into something new doesn't put you at risk, no matter how icky it feels. I can promise, though, that when you do step into that situation, and you come out unscathed, you will feel like a dolt for thinking it was scary in the first place. Anytime we take a step outside our comfort circle, the natural reaction is almost always, *well, that wasn't so bad.*

The beauty of stepping into resistance is that the more you do it, the easier it becomes. The next time a similar situation arises, you are far less likely to be worried about it, because you've been there, done that. Moving past the fears you have about your business really is as simple as that. Is it easy? No, not always, but it is simple.

Fear Is Weak

Fear is a bully, and when it sees you at your weak point, it will exploit that and nag at you. Fear will tease and taunt you because it knows exactly how to get at you, but there's a secret that most don't know. Fear is a little punk who talks tough but is a weak-sauce pissant. If you step to fear, it will back down every single time. If you show up in that situation that initially scared you, fear will turn tail and run. Fear puts on a good act, but understand that it is more scared of you than you are of it.

The resistance you feel when pushing into something new is a thin wall separating you from success. If you press your finger into a balloon, you feel the resistance, and the balloon pushes back at you, but use a needle, and that wall gives away in an instant. When you sense a fear in a situation, remember that you are a razor-sharp instrument, not a blunt object. You have the ability to do more damage than fear ever could. Fear should be afraid of you, but it puts on a good act. Will you be fooled by it?

Fear Is Boring

When you watch horror movies, do you root for the victims? Of course you don't. The only time you root for the people being hunted or attacked is when they stand up and fight for themselves. Jason Voorhees and Freddy Krueger have exponentially more fans than any of the victims in the movie. Even though they are scary dudes, they are strong, powerful, and not afraid of anything. They may be homicidal maniacs, but we love them.

Your fear is dull to others, but your strength is sexy. Confidence and tenacity are far more attractive than fear will ever be, and when you show up and do the things that you were afraid to do before, people will love you. Show people how you fought through something you were scared of and they will cheer you on. Several times over the past few years, I have written on my blog about coming into a situation that held me back, or where I hit a big obstacle. I could have backed down and gave up, but I chose to move forward, and share the story. Whenever I do this, I get tons of people commenting on how inspiring it is to hear about me fighting and winning. They are more eager to be a champion of my brand because they know I'm a fighter.

I don't talk about my fears from a place of scarcity, though. I express them, but I always talk about how I get past them. I am still human, and I battle fear as much as anyone. When I do, I share it, and people love to hear it, because it gives them hope for their own battle. They're not cheering about my admission of fear. They're cheering for the strength and courage. Be strong, push back against fear, share that story, and people will cheer for you too.

8

CONCLUSION

I'm not going to lie to you, that was a lot of information to drop in your lap, and you might feel totally overwhelmed right about now. The full scope of the content you just consumed could take days or weeks to absorb. Furthermore, adding these new tasks to your business practices will take even more of your precious time. If I wasn't the one who wrote it, I would think the author was a complete nut for putting all that on you. The truth is, though, what I have discussed in this book is the new reality we face as creative business owners.

This new world of selling our products, both online and off, has opened up many possibilities for independent artists, designers, and makers. We get the benefit of these new opportunities by being able to sell our work in a myriad of ways, and not be limited by the traditional business gatekeepers. Artists don't need galleries, clothing designers don't need boutiques, soap makers don't need beauty supply stores, and writers don't need bookstores in order to be successful. It's never been easier to get a business started, which is both a great thing, and a not-so-great thing. There are thousands upon thousands of people joining the ranks every single day, and it's only going to get more crowded.

At the same time, more and more people are becoming online shoppers every day. It's surprising to think about, but at the time of this writing, there are still fewer people on the Internet than people offline, but that is also changing daily. In the next few years, you will be able to sell to far more people than you do now, but so can your competitors. The difference of who makes the bigger impact will come down to how you present yourself to the world from now on, developing a brand people can trust.

The work you put into your branding development now may not pay overnight dividends, but if you stick to the path of telling good stories, making great things, and delivering them in beautiful ways, people will notice, and you will solidify a place in their hearts and minds as a brand worth investing in for years. It may not happen tomorrow, next week, next month, or next season, but your diligence and dedication to sharing the best parts of you and your products will bring in returns.

Start small, and build your brand over time. The important part is sticking to your plan, and not chasing all the different butterflies that come into view. For customers, new products and offerings are always sexy, but a brand that changes too often becomes frenetic and unreliable. It may be tempting to change up your graphics, colors, and subject matter in your social posts, but what customers really want is new products from reliable brands. That may sound boring or mundane, but consider some big brands you love and think about how often they change their branding. Successful brands stay current, topical, but consistent. The items they sell may be fashionable and trendy, but the branding is always on point—that is how they became a big brand. You may not want that level of success, but the lesson is still the same.

If you want to stay small, then by all means, stay small; incorporate that idea into your branding. If you own that idea, it can help you find your ideal customers. If you fake it, they will sense it, call you out—or worse, ignore you. Remain true to who you are internally, and what your work represents, and that will become the cornerstone of a brand that people rave about.

Take Good Care

The last little bit of insight I think is essential for you is to be kind to yourself. I have loaded you up with ideas and information. It's going to take time to build upon, and you may feel compelled to go crazy with all of it. Materials, media, Internet bandwidth, an even creativity are limitless—your health and well-being are not. I'm as much a workaholic as the next, um... workaholic, but I know it's important for me to take time for myself and my family.

A little scheduled decompression now and then will help you build a better business, whether that's a daily workout routine, a weekend away from work, or a simple spa day once in a while. If you're killing yourself slowly with work, eventually you may not want do to the work anymore, or worse, you may not have the ability to do the work.

You know when you fly in a jetliner, and the flight attendant runs down all the safety information? There's a part in that speech where they tell you about cabin decompression. In the event it happens, the oxygen masks fall from the ceiling, and if you are with someone incapable of putting theirs on, they tell you to put your mask on first. They do this because they don't want you passing out while attempting to put the mask on a toddler who fights it. Take care of yourself first, so you can take care of others after. You will have plenty of time to serve others once you get yourself in check.

With that last cautionary tale, I will leave you to your devices. Before I go, remember that I have complete faith in you, and what you can achieve. That may sound like lip service, but I believe it in my heart that if you put forth the effort to develop a business brand that matters, it will pay off for you. To walk my own talk, here is my email address: dc@daveconrey.com.com. That is a direct line to me, and not a gatekeeper (at least until I become super famous). You can reach out to me there anytime, or hit me up in social media—@daveconrey pretty much everywhere. If you have questions, are struggling with aspects of the book, or just want to reach and and talk shop, I'm always available. I can't always respond to emails in a timely fashion, but I try hard to get back to everyone.

You got this, and I believe that. Some of this may sound scary, and I don't doubt that resistance exists for you (it exists for all of us), but remember that every small step you take outside of your comfort circle expands that circle a little more, and each subsequent step becomes easier. Take that step, tell that story, and continue to build the most awesome brand you can. I promise, that is exactly what the world wants from you.

RESOURCES

These are the items and services I talk about in the book, along with a few extra that will help you with your productivity.

EMAIL SERVICES

MailChimp
This is the service I use for email newsletters. As a designer, I appreciate the easy-to-use interface, and it's simple for anyone to get started. It's also has a freemium pay scale that allows you to get started without shelling out any cash.

Aweber
I use to be an Aweber customer, but I was having trouble with my messages going out to my list. There is something to be said for Aweber's customer service, and they might be a better option for businesses with a large list (10k+ subscribers). Aweber is a paid service with different levels, depending on the options you need.

WEBSITE TOOLS & PLUGINS

Google Analytics
The analytics service of record for just about everyone. It's robust and totally free. What's not to love?

Clicky Analytics
An alternative analytics service for your website. People who use this resource say it offers more accurate data that's easier to understand than Google. However, Clicky is a paid service.

Jetpack
A plugin for WordPress-based websites that boosts functionality of your site, plus has some site-specific analytics. Jetpack is free and comes with each WordPress installation, but you must configure it.

Editorial Calendar Plugin
If you are a writer and want to plan out your blog-writing calendar, this WordPress plugin will help you get your schedule in check.

WEBSITE HOSTING

Bluehost
The hosting service I use for all my sites. I prefer Bluehost because they are inexpensive, yet offer all the amenities of pricier hosts. They have excellent support, and have simple one-click installation of Wordpress, which makes getting a website up and running super easy.

Squarespace
The beauty of using Squarespace as a platform is how easy it is to get an attractive site up and running. The user dashboard is more intuitive than some other content management services, and making changes to your site is simple. Being able to make design changes on the fly, without any formal coding knowledge, is remarkable. They also make it easy to incorporate a shop and newsletter opt-ins into your site. Compared to a self-hosted solutions like using Bluehost, Squarespace is pricier overall, but considering the flexibility and easy of use, it may be the right solution for you.

Shopify
If what you want is a turnkey solution to get your own online shop up and running with all your product offerings, with little need for tweaking, then Shopify might be your solution. This is the premier e-commerce solution for small businesses, and you pay for that status. The pricing is still reasonable, especially if you are selling plenty of product each month. If you're looking to step away from marketplaces like Etsy, Shopify is a suitable option.

PRODUCTIVITY

Typeform
This is one of the coolest services I've seen pop up recently. It allows you to create beautiful forms on the fly for a variety of needs. Need a contact form for you website, or a payment form so people can send you money for things? If you need to send a

questionnaire to your readers to ask them more about what they like, Typeform gives you that flexibility. Pretty much anytime you need to collect data from someone, Typeform can handle it, and with both free and paid models, you have plenty of flexibility.

Schedule Once

The scheduling tool I use for collaboration with others. Whether I'm scheduling a coaching call, or an interview for the podcast, this web-based app allows both parties to get appointments scheduled with ease. This is a paid app, but the cost is minimal.

SOCIAL MEDIA TOOLS

Hootsuite

This app has been around for a while, and hasn't changed all that much over the past few years, but that's because it's functionality was solid from the get-go. If you want to manage several social media accounts from one interface and be able to schedule posts so you can get in, get work done, and get back out again, then Hootsuite is your app. It's free to use, but you can upgrade to the premium account, which gets you a lot more functionality.

Edgar

This is another cool, new app that emerged in 2014. This site does one thing, and one thing only: It schedules posts in a way unlike any other app does. You can set up several channels and categories, import multiple posts to be recycled infinitely based on the schedule you put forth. For instance, every time you write a blog post, you can create an update in Meet Edgar, and that post will get recycled numerous times in succession along with all the other posts you put up. This helps keep your content relevant while allowing you freedom from hands-on updates in social media. Meet Edgar is a paid service and it's not cheap, but if it helps you gain more followers, more engagement, and free up your time, then it's worth the investment.

DESIGN & GRAPHICS

DaFont

If you're looking for a font to download free, check out DaFont. There are thousands upon thousands of fonts to choose from, all of them free. Not all fonts are created equal, though, and there is a LOT of crap on DaFont, so be choosy. Sometimes you get what you pay for when you use free fonts.

MyFonts
This is my go-to site for purchasing fonts. In fact, the font I'm using in this book is one I bought from MyFonts.com. Some might ask why I would buy fonts when I can get free ones on DaFont. It comes down to two things. First, the fonts you get on MyFonts are typically superior quality to what you find on DaFont. Second, I'm supporting the designers who make the fonts, which is a thankless effort because so many of them get their work stolen on a regular basis. I buy fonts for typographic karma.

The Dieline
As far as packaging goes, there is no better site for getting a handle on contemporary packaging design aesthetics. If you're looking to improve your product offering with a better package, check out The Dieline for inspiration.

BOOKS TO READ

Getting Things Done - David Allen
One of the most popular methods for attacking your productivity. David Allen's book has been around for several years now and it's still regarded as one of the best productivity tools around.

Making Ideas Happen - Scott Belsky
The title of this book pretty much explains the contents. This is all about taking your business or project and finding a way to turn it into a reality through a particular process created by the author over his many years and experiences. I encourage everyone to read this book to fully understand how the most productive individuals handle the overload.

Cultural Strategy - Douglas Holt
Want to know more about how small brands become big brands? This one will give you insights from some of the most notable corporate brands, and the driving factors behind their rise to prominence.

Thank You Economy - Gary Vaynerchuk

Whether you're a fan of @GaryVee or not, his thoughts on how brands thrive in the new digital economy are worth examining. His point of view is that if you provide massive value to your community, that community will be compelled to buy from you as a reward (a thank you) for all you have given them. Do good things—get good things in return.

COMMUNITY

Fresh Rag Army

This one is self-serving to a degree, but I created this group for all of you. I started seeing my reach on my Facebook page slipping, so I needed to do something about it. I started the group to reach people in a new way, plus also give them a way to interact with each other to promote, share, ask questions, and inform others of their specialization. Come join us.

CAN I ASK A FAVOR?

As a self-published author, I thrive on three things. First is sales (big surprise), second is referrals (share this with someone, would ya?), and third is ratings on Amazon.

It is my goal to provide so much value, you can't help but do great things with your business. At the very end of this book, you will have an opportunity to rate my effort and share your thoughts with the community. I want you to voice your opinions without falter, and I appreciate any thoughts you may have about what you read, so please share. Even slightly, unfavorable ratings are better than no ratings, so I welcome whatever you have to share.

That said, I hope you give it top marks, because that would be awesome. If you did enjoy it, please share it with your friends and family. Hopefully, we can keep this ball rolling, and change the landscape of how creative business owners treat themselves and their businesses. *Vive le créatif révolucion.*

www.daveconrey.com/rate-lac

ALSO BY DAVE CONREY

SELLING ART ONLINE
Your art deserves to be seen! If you're an artist, designer, illustrator, or photographer, *Selling Art Online* will help you find ways to get your art into the hands of more people. It's a comprehensive look at various platforms where you can share your work, as well as business fundamentals for taking your work to the next level.

www.daveconrey.com/saobook

DAVECONREY.COM
If you'd like to get more awesomeness delivered right to your inbox, get in on the newsletter list. Each week, I deliver tips, techniques, insights, and stories about things I have found that make creative businesses thrive. Also, newsletter subscribers get first dibs on new content, and get special deals that others do not get.

www.daveconrey.com

THE FRESH RAG SHOW
Can't get enough Dave in your life? How about having me direct into your eardrums each week? *The Fresh Rag Show* is a weekly (or more) podcast where I sit down with today's most compelling creatives to share their stories and insights. These conversations are not to be missed.

www.freshrag.com

ABOUT THE AUTHOR

Dave Conrey is an author, artist, and podcaster. When not spending time playing dinosaurs and robots with his son, he is working on a number of creative projects, ranting on his podcast, or writing his next book.

Before launching his own brand, he worked for two decades as a marketing professional and art director, and he uses this experience to inform, engage, and advise creative entrepreneurs on how to take their work from a hobby to a viable business. Visit daveconrey.com to get updates on everything he is working on.

LIFE
AFTER
CHRIST
MAS